Henry Augustus Boardman

Mottoes for the New Year

As given in Texts of Sermons preached in the Tenth Presbyterian Church,

Philadelphia

Henry Augustus Boardman

Mottoes for the New Year
As given in Texts of Sermons preached in the Tenth Presbyterian Church, Philadelphia

ISBN/EAN: 9783337116538

Printed in Europe, USA, Canada, Australia, Japan

Cover: Foto ©ninafisch / pixelio.de

More available books at **www.hansebooks.com**

MOTTOES FOR THE NEW YEAR,

AS GIVEN IN TEXTS OF SERMONS

PREACHED IN THE

TENTH PRESBYTERIAN CHURCH,

PHILADELPHIA.

BY

HENRY A. BOARDMAN, D.D.

PHILADELPHIA:
E. CLAXTON AND COMPANY,
No. 930 Market Street.
1882.

COLLINS, PRINTER.

This volume of Sermons for the New Year is offered to the people of Dr. Henry A. Boardman's charge with certain anticipation of its welcome. During his long ministry they often desired the publication of such of his addresses as had been particularly instructive and acceptable, and to this disposition to preserve what is of special intrinsic value is now added the influence of their reverent and regretful recollection. These Sermons were respectively greeted with marked interest as the period for them arrived, and Dr. Boardman was repeatedly asked to publish them. But the time never came when he could comply with this wish of several of his friends, and give to his people a course of sermons extending over a period of fifteen years, and of a character to renew in each coming year its rich offering of pertinent suggestion and comforting assurance.

The general oneness of the subjects here proposed, and the character of the texts, brief, simple, practical, have limited to some extent the preacher's varied power, and induced, though moderately, a repetition of sentiment and method which in a more miscellaneous series could not occur. Yet, among these discourses there are several which may fairly take rank with others that, prepared for extraordinary occasions, or discussing some favorite topic, were looked upon as models of treatment, and in their various published forms will remain precious and permanent possessions to Dr. Boardman's friends, his people, and the Church.

To a wider Christian and literary public these Sermons can be commended with almost equal confidence. They are the utterances of a man whose name and opinions are not now for the first time before the reading world, awaiting doubtfully its award. Long ago his reputation as a writer, a speaker, a Christian teacher, was fully established, and on some questions his judgment had come to be considered, in more than one large circle, as substantially ultimate. His statements and arguments went forth with authority, accredited always, whether altogether accepted or not, as the result of sound mental processes, and of rarely cautious and candid investigation. The quality of his expression was thought by competent and impartial critics to bear ready comparison with that of any writer of the day in our country. So decided was his intellectual ability, so generous was his culture, so accurate was his habit, so delicate his discrimination, that he could not but deal as a master with any subject that came within his range, nor fail to attain in his own department to the high distinction of a faithful interpreter and zealous guardian of Scriptural truth.

But, more than this: the facts and teachings of the word of God were accepted by Dr. Boardman with an entireness and energy of assent, with a freshness of individual perception, and with an immediate influence on the inner man, that eminently qualified him to speak as a messenger of the Gospel of Jesus Christ. It was *the grace of God* in his heart, and that Divine fulness, wherever it is received, will press itself forth in free and beneficent overflow. There must be, then, a bountiful supply in these Sermons for the many in every Christian denomination who are always eager to draw counsel and consolation from Gospel sources: and, surely, a candid hearing will again be given to words so solemn in their import, so discerning of men's spiritual needs, so faithful, so kindly, so persuasive,—words that truly indicate, as they earnestly recommend, a large Christian attainment and a complete self-surrender to the Redeemer and his cause.

Whatever expectation as to the local and general acceptance of this tribute to his memory, our estimate of Dr. Boardman's character and services may lead us to form, we bear in mind that his controlling desire in publishing, as in preaching, was to proclaim as widely, and in as many of its gracious aspects, as he might, the Gospel of Jesus Christ, the Son of God. May the Holy Spirit incline each reader to give to these maxim truths their rightful place in the system of his faith, and to acknowledge their Divine authority in the daily conduct of his life!

S.

December, 1881.

CONTENTS.

		PAGE
I.	GOD IS MINE HELPER. Psalm liv. 4,	9
II.	THE LORD IS AT HAND. Philippians iv. 5,	27
III.	"I WILL REJOICE IN THE LORD." Habakkuk iii. 18, .	43
IV.	"THIS IS MY FRIEND." Song of Solomon v. 16,	61
V.	"FOR TO ME TO LIVE IS CHRIST." Philippians i. 21, .	79
VI.	"WAITING FOR THE COMING OF OUR LORD JESUS CHRIST." 1 Corinthians i. 7,	95
VII.	"APPROVED UNTO GOD." 2 Timothy ii. 15,	113
VIII.	"TO EVERY MAN HIS WORK." Mark xiii. 34,	135
IX.	"THIS IS NOT YOUR REST." Micah ii. 10,	155
X.	"MY GRACE IS SUFFICIENT FOR THEE." 2 Corinthians xii. 9,	175
XI.	"I AM WITH THEE." Isaiah xli. 10, .	193
XII.	"A LITTLE WHILE." John xvi. 16,	211
XIII.	"THE LORD WILL GIVE GRACE AND GLORY." Psalm lxxxiv. 11,	233
XIV.	"WHOSE I AM, AND WHOM I SERVE." Acts xxvii. 23, .	253

1858.

I.

GOD IS MINE HELPER.

PSALM LIV. 4.

SINCE we last met in this place, we have interchanged the customary social congratulations on the advent of a New Year. We are here to recognize this event in a more formal manner, and in some of its more important aspects. The anniversary is one which is sure to commingle in its observance our hopes and our regrets. The sorrows and the sins of the year that is gone are but too certain to come thronging around us, while, with equal certainty, our aspirations will go forth in quest of something purer and better in the future. Each successive year admonishes us afresh how absolute is our ignorance of the future. 'Thou knowest not what shall be on the morrow.' Much less canst thou forecast the changes which may be evolved before we, or others in our place, shall meet here on another New Year's Sabbath.

But one thing we do know:—If God be for us, we have nothing to fear from those who may be against us. In this view, I propose with all respect and affection, to give you something to think of during the coming twelvemonth. You may call it, if you will, your *Year-text*, or your *Motto for the Year*. Perhaps there is many a scene and event before you in which it will comfort you to recall the words, "God is mine helper." It was this reflection which cheered the heart of David when pursued by his enemies, and in peril of his life. It may solace and strengthen you also in time of trouble.

This, however, is but a very partial view of the use I would have you make of this Scripture. You all understand the design of a motto. The one I venture to suggest to you will be found as comprehensive as, to every Christian heart, it must be animating.

'God is mine Helper.' I can conceive of no equipment better than this for launching forth upon the pathless expanse of a new year. The forty-sixth Psalm has long gone in the Church by the name of Luther's Psalm, because the great Reformer was accustomed to repair to it for succor in all emergencies:—'God is our refuge and strength, a very present help in trouble.' Not less cheering will you find the assurance, 'God is mine Helper.'

I have characterized it as 'comprehensive.' So varied are the occasions upon which it may be invoked, and so numerous the ends to which it can fairly be applied, that I should exhaust your patience by attempting anything like a complete discussion of the subject. All you will expect or desire of me is some passing illustrations of the use to be made of this promise in the ordinary experiences of life.

The offer of 'help' directs the mind intuitively to our need of help, and the proper answer to the inquiry, 'When do we require help?' is, 'When do we not require it?' Sinful, wayward, and suffering creatures, our necessities are as continued as the moments of our lives. Our Saviour spoke without a figure when he said, 'Without me ye can do nothing.' In all our duties, all our trials, all our temptations, all our pleasures, we need help from above. If there are any who think otherwise, this fact itself only shows how great their real need is.

With every thoughtful person this season is sure to awaken reflections on the proper ends of life, and the manner in which we are fulfilling them. It is well, at the opening of a year, to endeavor to frame a just estimate of our own powers and opportunities, and of the objects for which we are living. How common and how disastrous it is to err on these points, appears to every one who casts an eye over society. Everywhere we see a sad inversion of things,—the higher interests subordinated to the inferior, time made paramount to eternity, and earth to heaven. Even with ourselves, very much of life may have been a mistake. And where its aims have been right, they have too often been pursued with languor and inconstancy. How little have we, any of us, to shew for life, as compared with what we should have! How meagre the results of our twenty, thirty, fifty years!

Perhaps we have been at fault in our plans; or, we have misjudged our own capacities and responsibilities; or we have disparaged the aids proffered us by our Heavenly Father. If there is any disposition to revise the scheme of life, and to get a new and juster view of it, you need not lack for an infallible Teacher. 'GOD is mine Helper.' This will meet your case. For the help He affords is not confined to the exigencies of outward duty or suffering. It is his prerogative, no less, to illuminate the understanding and to control the working of all our intellectual forces.

And herein, by the way, we are reminded of one of the most interesting of the methods in which He is wont to vindicate the implied promise of the text. There is no pursuit in which we more imperatively require his aid than in the *search after truth*. This is an employment worthy of our rational nature. For truth, like its Author, is immutable. It is the prescribed aliment of the soul,—that by which it must be nourished and expanded, and which can never cease to be its portion and its life. But it does not obtrude itself upon the inert and the careless. Even in a sinless realm, the acquisition of truth no doubt requires exertion. And to us it is like treasure *hid* in a field. Especially is this the case as regards religious truth. Here, there is a veil upon our minds which no human hand can lift. And then the difficulties are largely increased by the variety of creeds and sects, and the conflicting interpretations put upon the sacred oracles. No one who considers these things can refuse his sympathy to those who are reverently and patiently asking, 'What is truth?'

It is quite certain that this search after truth will engage, in the course of the present year, the attention of many who are now before me. You will be seeking after the way to the cross; or you will be striving after a clearer insight into the doctrines of grace; or you will be bringing opinions you have long held to the touchstone of the law and the testimony. And, whatever direction your inquiries may take, you will not fail to draw encouragement from the assurance, 'God is mine Helper.'

He is the Helper of all who seek in sincerity to learn his will. He has promised to be their Teacher. It is one of the express offices of his Spirit, to guide us into the truth. Let this dwell upon your minds whenever, as this year passes on, you sit down to the study of the Bible, or when you listen to the preaching of the Gospel. The passages from which you can extract no satisfactory meaning will become, under the Spirit's teaching, as lucid as the sunbeam; and the doctrines which embarrass or distress you, will be found not only Scriptural but comforting. Thus instructed, you will grow in the knowledge of Jesus Christ. Your faith will rest upon broader foundations; and, with a more comprehensive view of the perfections and government of God, you will have enlarged your sources of pure and elevated enjoyment.

We may pass beyond the sphere of religious inquiries. While there is a special significance with which we may say, in prosecuting these studies, 'God is mine Helper,' we need not, and should not, exclude his agency from studies of a less spiritual character. You have devoted yourselves, it may be, to the cause of Science. To whatever point in this wide domain you may have directed your attention, it would ill become you to decline the aid of the "Spirit of truth." Genuine philosophy is the handmaid of genuine piety. With equal capacities and opportunities, they will ordinarily be most successful in their researches who pursue them in a spirit of reverence and gratitude towards the Supreme Being. He rewards the devout student of nature, as He does the devout student of his word, with discoveries which are concealed from the eyes of the self-complacent and the profane. The Geologist who traces in the vegetation of the rocks the memorials of the Creator's wisdom; the Botanist who sees in every bud and blossom the image of Him who has made the lilies of the field a sweet remembrancer of their Lord; the Astronomer who walks among the glories of the firmament only to adore the brighter glories of Him who set the stars in their courses and calls them by their names;—all these may fitly say, 'God is mine Helper.'

Nor these alone. There can be no better motto for the Professional man than this. The grand aim of the liberal professions, like the ultimate end of all Science, is truth. And here also Truth hides herself, and must be sought out with arduous and patient toil. The intricacies of the Law, for example, are proverbial. The service laid upon the Bar, involves the interpretation of abstruse and ambiguous statutes, the examination of reluctant or reckless witnesses, the parrying of adverse arguments, the harmonizing or annulling of precedents, the application of settled principles to facts, and, generally, a course of procedure in which there is ample room, as well for the loftiest exertion of intellect, as for the play of those fervid passions and sympathies which constitute so essential and intractable a part of our being. Through all this complexity of influences the lawyer must make his way, not in quest of truth as a metaphysical abstraction, but in quest of Truth as the sponsor of invaluable personal rights, as the guardian of men's property or liberty, or, possibly, of life itself. No man can hope to compass the just demands of this noble profession without exhausting labor. But even this needs to be reinforced from without. And with every Christian lawyer—Christian, not in name and form merely, but in heart and life—there is the unfailing support which is bound up in the feeling, 'God is mine Helper.'

Is there any reason why this feeling should not be carried into all the activities and conflicts of the forum? The promise, 'I will help thee,' is not limited to sacred times and places, and to the offices of religion. The same Providence directs as well our secular as our spiritual affairs. If whether we eat or drink, or whatever we do, we are to do all to the glory of God, then must we be warranted to look for his assistance in every lawful occupation and in every scene of duty. It is one of the bright anticipations we associate with the coming millennium, that all professions will then be conducted on the high principles of Scripture morality, and pervaded with the spirit of the Gospel. When "Holiness to the Lord" comes to be inscribed upon the bells of the horses, Christianity will no longer be denied its rightful place in the social structure. It is cause for congratulation that its claims are now acknowledged by so many whose abilities adorn the walks of jurisprudence. In their loyalty to Christ they are consulting their own good, professional as well as spiritual. For the promise is, 'Them that honor me, I will honor.' On the ground of success in life, a young lawyer would do well to plant himself upon the deep foundations of Christianity. But there are loftier motives by far which should prompt to this course; and those who adopt it will know the strength and the comfort to be drawn from that scripture, 'God is mine Helper.'

If the Jurist requires this, how much more the Physician. With him, the stake is not property nor liberty, but life. The enemy he has to cope with is subtle and insidious; entrenched, often, in the hiding-places of the system, and skilful in masking his true character. We need not disguise the fact:—while Medicine justly claims its position as a science, there must still be very much in the application of it which can only be referred to conjecture and experiment. This is no disparagement of the Profession. Man cannot achieve impossibilities, and the age of miracles is past. We accept the Science as it is, and recognize in it one of the greatest of our temporal blessings. We note with gratitude the signal progress it is making. But we are daily reminded that it is overmastered even by familiar diseases. And when we see a physician grappling with maladies on the issue of which precious lives are suspended, and, with them, the happiness and hopes of a wide circle of friends and kindred, we feel that if there be any earthly mission in which men need help from heaven, it is this. It cannot be deemed surprising, in this view, that families should so often desire the ministrations of a Christian physician. It is not merely that they confide in the integrity which has religion for its basis, and understand that personal piety is the nurse of delicacy and sympathy, but that the conviction forms and strengthens that such a physician carries the blessing of God with him.

We cannot err in supposing, that he himself, as he pursues his daily rounds among the sick and the dying, must appreciate, as few other men can, the assurance, 'God is mine Helper.' Let the young men who have devoted themselves to Medicine think of this. On a strictly professional view of the subject, nothing could more enhance the value of your attainments, or better aid you in making a successful use of them, than a personal faith in Jesus Christ. It will be a rare element of professional power, if, when you have entered upon your work, you shall be able to say, day after day, as you go forth to the abodes of disease and suffering, 'God is mine Helper.' And when you superadd the considerations proper to your individual accountability, and the obligations which lie upon you, as upon each one of us, to do all that can be done for the Church of Christ and the good of mankind, how can you think of ever engaging in the practice of this most beneficent profession without first consecrating yourself to the service of God?

As I look over this congregation my sympathies are enlisted, as they have long been, in behalf of the Men of Business here. It were superfluous to talk to you of the hazards and vexations which are bound up in a business life. You know more about them than I could tell you. And the present season is one, above all others, to enforce the lesson with which I come to you to-day. It is while the remembrance of these great disasters is fresh upon your minds that I would remind you of the only Source from which you can ever derive help commensurate with your necessities. Calamities which overwhelm men, which break up their plans, and disperse their fortunes, occur only at intervals. But all along the thoroughfares of business, there are temptations and discomforts which try the temper and, sometimes, imperil the soul. It must happen very often in the course of a year that when you return to your homes at evening your retrospect of the day will include some passage of an irksome or painful character—some provocation given or taken, some injury inflicted or received, or something which you would gladly efface from the record.

Now it were fanciful to imagine that there is any infallible method by which all experiences of this sort can be avoided. They inhere more or less in the kind of life you are leading. But what cannot be cured, may at least be mitigated. I do not say, that the text is a talisman which will carry you harmless through all temptations and perplexities. But if you could only have the sentiment, 'God is mine Helper' deeply enshrined in your hearts and guarded by a firm faith, it will certainly enable you to go on your way with a steadier step, and to lift your eyes in surrounding darkness to the true Light which lighteth every man that cometh into the world.

Suppose you take it with you to your counting-rooms, your factories, and your workshops, morning by morning, and see whether there is not in it virtue to purify the atmosphere you breathe through the day. Two great ideas it embosoms, God, and Help. It must be useful to have these before the mind anywhere. If the thought of God were more familiar in the realm of trade, it would be auspicious for the eager crowd who jostle each other in its avenues. The mistake lies in excluding the Deity from this realm; in assigning religion to its place, and traffic to its place, and keeping up an unscriptural and vicious divorce between them. Surely you cannot dispense with Christianity in your business. You need its principles, you need its counsels, you need its comforts. It can aid you as no earthly power can. Accept the succor it tenders you, and carry it with you as '*vade mecum*,' your inseparable guide and support through the year— 'God is mine Helper.'

And what better maxim can be proposed for the secluded world of Home? The cares, the trials, the joys, the temptations, the anxieties, the pleasures of Household life—what pencil can delineate this variegated scene, with its ever-shifting lights and shadows? And who does not feel his own incompetency to deal with its responsibilities? Next to keeping one's own heart, there is scarcely anything harder to do than to bring up a family of children aright. 'Aright,' I say; for, of course, they are brought up in some way. But how this duty is too commonly performed, it needs but a glance around us to show. The difficulties attending it demand an amount of wisdom and patience, of love and firmness, which only a few parents possess. And even these are frequently baffled by questions unexpectedly evolved out of even ordinary and daily family life, or lost sight of in sudden shadows which envelop the household in gloom.

That any parent can be willing to bear such a burden without the aid of religion may well awaken surprise. Even a true faith may not be equal to all the emergencies of this relation. But there is certainly no other resource which offers so much assistance, and supplies so much encouragement, as the presence and blessing of God. I will not say to you, Hang up this precious Scripture in your parlors, in your bed-chambers, in your libraries. But I will say to you, Grave it upon the palms of your hands, and upon the tablets of your hearts, 'God is mine Helper.' Bear it with you into the familiar scenes of every-day life. Have it within reach every moment. This year will bring with it occasions when you will feel your need of it. It may evoke many an ejaculatory prayer to the Giver of all good, keep you from many an error in judgment, repress many an unseemly ebullition of temper, and carry you safely through many a scene of perplexity. Be it your household motto, 'God is mine Helper.'

It has already been intimated that this exclamation broke from David's lips, when he was in peril of his life. The most obvious association it suggests, is that of *trouble* or *danger*. And since we are all exposed to afflictions, it would seem to be both reasonable and important that we prepare for them. This year will tread the beaten round of the years that have preceded it. Sickness and sorrow and change will come, as they have been wont to come, and do their allotted work. Families that are now in affluence may see their riches make to themselves wings and fly away. Families that are now given up to unthinking gaiety, may be clad in mourning. Some who are to-day in health will die. Others will lose their health, and fall into the sad routine which defines the life of an invalid. Parents will still be tried by the follies and the sins of their children. Whatever else may fail, trouble will not forego its mission. Where, or in what shape, it may come, no finite mind may presume to say. But that its foot-prints will be seen here on the next new year's day, in places where they are not seen now, and, in some instances, freshly made where they are seen now, no one can for a moment hesitate to believe.

Can you wonder, then, if you are urged to make this pledge of sympathy and protection your own? We are none of us able to cope with affliction in our own strength. Men of obtuse sensibilities may bear trouble without heeding it. Natural fortitude or pride may do something towards sustaining an individual under it. But in neither case is there anything in the deportment worthy of our rational nature, and of the relations we sustain to God. Affliction is his rod. He never uses it without a purpose. He means that we shall feel it. To be indifferent to it, or to bear it with a proud and sullen acquiescence, is an affront to Him. Christian resignation is as alien from this carriage as light from darkness. There can be no true submission except as He imparts it. Nor can we have any adequate support in seasons of trial except that which comes from Him.

'God is mine Helper!' What could mourners do without this? The shafts of death are falling around us, smiting here a blooming infant, there a man of threescore and ten, and there a youth in the pride and flush of early manhood;—what are these stricken households to do if they cannot say 'God is my Helper!' And what other dependence have these invalids, to whom are allotted weary months of debility and suffering? Even if their trial be not aggravated by the woes of poverty, and they enjoy the alleviations which wealth can command, and the soothing ministry of attached friends, these cannot satisfy them. They need something which they can hope for unvaryingly; something which can make them see that it is a Father's hand that is leading them along this thorny path; something which can disarm death of its sting, and reveal to them a risen Saviour and a reconciled God; something which can fill their souls with peace and patience, and, as their sufferings abound, cause their consolations to superabound. This 'something' earth has not to give. It is bound up in the sweet assurance, 'God is mine Helper.'

There are those here who have found it so. I have but rehearsed to you their experience. And an experience it is of so much higher value than anything of earth that I should only degrade it by comparing it with gold and silver, or thrones and sceptres. Is not the bare statement of the case sufficient to commend their example to your imitation? Rest assured it will be a privilege and blessing above all price if you shall be able to say, when disappointment and suffering come, 'God is mine Helper.' For in the Lord Jehovah is everlasting strength; and with his arms around you, you cannot sink. The storm may rage, and the billows swell, and your frail bark may strain and quiver, but if Christ be with you what have you to fear? He has but to say to the surging waves, 'Peace; Be Still!' and a calm like that which soothed the boisterous Gennesareth will spread itself through your agitated breast. That soul can have nothing to dread which has heard those wondrous words, 'Fear not, for I am with thee: Be not dismayed, for I am thy God.' Happy will it be for us if, as this year wears on and we encounter its trials, we can say with an humble and steadfast faith, 'God is mine Helper.'

Still more, if possible, shall we need this succor in our *spiritual conflicts*. If we cannot wage the warfare with sorrow in our own strength, much less can we carry on our warfare with sin. Here, above all others, is the field where we are made conscious of our impotence.

'Deny thyself, and take thy cross,
Is the Redeemer's great command.'

His 'great command' it is; and great is the difficulty of obeying it. Outward hinderances and dangers may be formidable, but they are not peculiar to the Christian life. And if they were, this would still remain 'the *great* command,'—'If any man will come after me, let him deny himself, and take up his cross daily, and follow me.' The grand requisition of Christianity is a discipline which amounts to self-crucifixion. It begins with the first earnest aspiration of the sinner to be freed from his bondage. It terminates only with the believer's expiring breath. The whole field he traverses in making his way to the celestial city has to be fought over, step by step. And the discouraging thing about it is that he carries his worst adversaries in his own bosom. It is himself he has to contend against; himself that is to be subdued; himself that has to be crucified. What wonder that even the great Apostle of the Gentiles, holy as he was, and honored of God and man as he was, should be so harassed by this warfare as to exclaim, 'Oh wretched man that I am, who shall deliver me from the body of this death!'

This contest is before us all—all except those who are content to submit themselves to the unchallenged and brutal mastery of their corrupt passions. The sins we have to struggle with may vary with our temperaments, our training, and our circumstances. With some they will have acquired a colossal strength, while with others they may be comparatively feeble or already brought into partial subjection. But in every case the final issue must depend upon the aid received from above. No one, not even the most mature and stable Christian, can stand before the power and subtlety of his own sins, except as an Almighty arm holds him up.

All along the paths before us there are temptations and snares correspondent with our several characters and occupations. Could the curtain be withdrawn from this year, as it now is from the year just closed, it would make us tremble to discover what perils await our souls, and how deadly and exhausting a contest we must have with our besetting sins before we can attain true peace of mind. Especially would it fill us with anxiety should we learn, as we might, that this year was to close the strife and determine our everlasting destiny.

Is it possible, in this aspect of things, to exaggerate the importance and the seasonableness of the Scripture with which we have to do? The exigences of this warfare are upon us. We cannot escape it. The true question with us all must be, 'How can I meet it?' And how *can* we meet it, except in the strength of Omnipotence? If we can but say, 'God is mine Helper,' all will be well. We may say of this motto, what Constantine said of the sign of the cross, which, according to the tradition, he saw in the air, and then placed upon his banner,—'*In hoc signo vinces:*' "By this sign thou shalt conquer." With a covenant God for our Defender, we need not fear the assaults of earth or hell, or the more dangerous corruption and treachery of our own hearts. The conflict may be severe and protracted, but its issue is as certain as it will be glorious. "Mine enemies would daily swallow me up: for they be many that fight against me, O thou most High. What time I am afraid I will trust in thee." "When I cry unto thee, then shall mine enemies turn their back: this I know; for God is for me." "Unto thee, O my strength, will I sing: for God is my defence, and the God of my mercy."

Such, then, is the divine equipment with which I would have you go forth to the duties and temptations, the trials and pleasures, of another year. To show wherein God is accustomed to 'help' his people, how willing he is to do it, in what manner his aid is to be sought, would exceed our allotted time. Nor can these points require elucidation to those who know what it is to trust in him. Enough, that it is the ineffable privilege of every one of his children to carry the assurance into all the avocations and events of life, 'God is mine Helper.'

Take it as your pastor's New-Year's wish and prayer, *May God be your Helper throughout this opening year!* May he help you, in joy and in sorrow, in sickness and in health. May He help you in poverty and in affluence, in your successes and in your reverses. May He help you in all your efforts to subdue your sins, and all your exertions to promote the prosperity of his Church and the salvation of your fellow-creatures. May He help you in fulfilling your daily duties, and in bearing your daily burdens. May He help you in submitting to trials without murmuring, and in enduring wrongs without resentment; in receiving mercies without ingratitude, and in enjoying this life without forgetting the life to come. May He help you in denying sinful self and in denying righteous self; in growing up into His image and putting on all the graces of the Spirit. May He help you in preparing for whatever He is preparing for you. And if it be so, that this is the last New Year's Sabbath you are to spend on earth, may the dawn of another year find you enjoying that Sabbath whose sun never goes down, and whose worship shall never end!

1859.

II.

THE LORD IS AT HAND.

PHILIPPIANS iv. 5.

In my last New Year's sermon I endeavored to recommend to you a certain text of scripture as your motto for the year. That text, 'God is mine Helper,' has so often recurred to my own mind with its lessons of encouragement and comfort, that I cannot but believe it has been a source of consolation to many of my people also. You will not think it strange, then, that on the occurrence of this anniversary, I should offer you a motto for the opening year.

'The Lord is at hand.' It is not certain what was the precise import of these words, as used by the apostle. The commentators are generally agreed that by 'the Lord' is intended the Lord Jesus Christ, not simply the Supreme Being. His being 'at hand' may be interpreted either of time or of place. Both senses give a good signification, and both are in accordance with the teaching of the Bible. By virtue of His Deity, He is present with all his creatures; as well a God at hand as a God afar off. And this thought would not be inapposite to the tenor of the context. But as similar expressions are repeatedly used in the New Testament to denote an actual coming of the Saviour to our world, the phrase is to be referred rather to time than to place. Of those expressions, again, some refer to the day of judgment; others to his providential coming for the overthrow of Jerusalem; and others still to the death of believers. Thus, we read, 'The coming of the Lord draweth nigh.' 'Yet a little while, and he that shall come, will come and will not tarry.' 'Who may abide in the day of his coming, and who shall stand when he appeareth?' The apostle James makes use of this consideration by way of comforting Christians under oppression: 'Be ye also patient; stablish your hearts: for the coming of the Lord draweth nigh.'

Without stopping to ascertain the exact meaning of the phrase in these several places, we shall not mistake seriously if we accept the text as referring to the coming of Christ to the judgment; or, what is practically the same thing, his coming to the soul at death.

For the purposes of the present discourse, however, we need not exclude the other idea of place. I would have you take the expression in a popular way, as we are wont to do with mottoes,—not refining upon the terms, but using it with freedom as a sentiment to be taken with you into all the scenes and through all the changes which this year may bring with it.

'The Lord is at hand!' If we could suppose this to be written upon our hearts by the Spirit of God, and kept there in its freshness and vigor, how powerful and how salutary the influence it would exert upon us during the coming twelvemonth, or for as much of that period as it may please God to spare us. Let us illustrate this thought.

The present is the season at which most persons frame their plans for the year. Speaking without regard to particular occupations, how different will your plans and aims be according as you admit into your calculations, or exclude, this one element! With a lively apprehension of the fact that 'The Lord is at hand,' your entire scheme of life will be one thing; without it, it will be a radically different thing. For this sentiment, affiliated as it is with others of like significance, must be of potent agency in any mind which embraces it. It is stamped with too much importance and too much solemnity to lie inert, like a mathematical axiom. Its proper effect is to bring the soul into the presence of eternity, to gather around it the sublime realties of the invisible world, and to reveal the indissoluble connection which subsists between our daily experiences and the issues of the life to come. Only believe that 'The Lord is at hand,' and you will consent to no scheme of effort which is defiled with the taint of practical atheism. Nothing will satisfy you but a plan which proceeds upon the morality of the Bible, which devoutly recognizes a universal Providence, and which contemplates, as its ultimate ends, the glory of God and the well-being of your fellow-creatures.

In this view, our year-text may be commended to persons of all classes and conditions. But there may be those here who are forming, not merely their plans for the year, but their plans for life; and to these the text proffers its friendly aid with an urgency which ought not to be declined. '*How can I make the most of life?*'— this is the question which stirs your bosoms, as it well may. For it is not a question to be trifled with. To evade it, to decide it carelessly, or to weigh it only in the scales of an earthly expediency, would be a grievous sin. We are all sent into the world upon a specific mission. We have a work to do for God. Our talents and acquirements, our resources and opportunities, are from Him. And it is his equitable demand that we employ them in his service. To choose one's profession or occupation without regard to this principle, savors of impiety, and forbids all hope of his blessing. But there would be little danger of mistake on this point with one whose habitual feeling is 'The Lord is at hand.' The idea that we were soon to stand at his bar and give an account of all the deeds done in the body, would be an effectual counterpoise to those selfish or, at least, purely secular considerations by which we are so apt to be swayed in deciding questions of duty. In fact, questions of duty are treated too much as if they were merely questions of convenience, or questions of profit and loss, or questions of self-aggrandizement. Let the young men who are present ponder this matter, and beware lest they fall into a disastrous error,—one which will give a false bias to their whole future career, and leave them at last with nothing to show for life but fruitless regrets and bitter self-reproaches.

No less apposite would this motto be in respect to the *actual prosecution* of our several callings. If it has a lesson for those who are deciding upon a profession, or maturing arrangements for life of a different kind, it teaches with equal cogency in what spirit our several tasks should be carried forward. For one thing, it rebukes our sloth and inefficiency. The proper sequence to the sentiment, 'The Lord is at hand,' is 'Life *in earnest.*' How little there is of this, especially in the sphere of religion, it needs but a glance to see. And yet the quality of earnestness is one which commands universal respect. Every one is attracted to an earnest man, even though he be earnest in a matter with which we cannot sympathize. But for the most part, we pursue our work, if not with leaden feet, yet with a loitering, truant industry, which seems to imply that life is long and sure. There is probably no one here who can review the year just closed without feeling that he might, with the ordinary blessing of Providence, have accomplished far more during that year than he now has to show for it. In the way of self-improvement; in the way, possibly, of your business; in the way of doing good both to the souls and the bodies of your fellow-creatures; you might have had a very different retrospect from that which a too faithful memory brings before you. It may save us from the renewal of these reproaches hereafter, should we enter upon the new year with the feeling deeply inwrought into our minds, 'The Lord is at hand!' For if this conviction be lodged in the heart, it will help to keep us mindful of the responsibility we are under to God for the diligent cultivation of all our powers, and the faithful performance of all our duties.

Nor, in respect to the secularities of life, would it tell simply upon these habits. It would be no less an incentive to truthfulness and integrity. The paths of business are thickly strewn with temptations. Men are continually dealing with questions of practical morality in the presence of their own pecuniary interest, and this enforced, it may be, by urgent want or by the sense of impending bankruptcy. What wonder that their honesty should often prove unequal to the strain thus put upon it? that concealment and deception and double-dealing should abound so much throughout the wide realm of traffic? The busy actors in that realm need to be fortified against these enticements. For it is a perilous thing, even to the best of men, to have to do all the while with money. Eighteen centuries ago it was written by an unerring pen, 'The love of money is the root of all evil.' And a thousand years before that, the wisest and richest man of the age, or perhaps of any age, had written 'The getting of treasures by a lying tongue is a vanity tossed to and fro of them that seek death.' And going back still further, Gehazi, with the costly vestments he obtained by fraud from Naaman, and Achan with his wedge of gold, and Lot with his broad acres in the well-watered vale of Sodom, and many others chronicled in Holy Writ, come forward to illustrate the warnings addressed to us on this subject. He, therefore, is not a wise man who, being shut up by Providence to the snares which are embosomed in a life of merchandise or a life of handicraft, declines any safeguard which may help to protect him from these dangers. And among such adjuvants, he would find it of no trivial assistance to remember, day by day, that 'The Lord is at hand.' The conviction of this truth would do much both to inspire him with a just estimate of the value of money, and to preserve him from unwarrantable expedients for the acquisition of it. Let the men of business who hear me, inscribe upon the walls of their counting-rooms and their workshops, 'The Lord is at hand,' and it will, by God's grace, carry them safely through many a temptation which might otherwise conquer them.

But we may go beyond the thoroughfares of business and generalize this idea. Could every heart be imbued with this feeling, it would do much to rectify that mal-arrangement of things which sin has occasioned in the affairs of our world. By the force of a fatal introversion, darkness is now put for light, and light for darkness. Time takes precedence of eternity. The things which are seen overshadow the things which are not seen. And earth absorbs the homage and the toil, the love and the devotion, which belong to God. Were it properly felt that 'The Lord is at hand,' all human interests would put on a different aspect. With the light of eternity let in upon our present abode, the plans which terminate here, and the common objects of ambition among men, would dwindle into their true insignificance. The riches which make to themselves wings and fly away, and the fame which lives upon the caprices of the populace, would be regarded as unworthy the supreme regard of a rational nature. Religion would rise to something of its real importance in the general estimation. Men would freely admit that it was 'the one thing needful.' And no exertions would be deemed too great, no sacrifices too costly, which might be demanded for the acquisition of its unspeakable blessings.

In the two brief Epistles of St. Peter, this argument is repeatedly used as an incentive to Christian steadfastness and perseverance. "But the end of all things is at hand: be ye therefore sober, and watch unto prayer." "Nevertheless we, according to his promise, look for new heavens and a new earth wherein dwelleth righteousness. Wherefore, beloved, seeing ye look for such things, be diligent that ye may be found of him in peace, without spot and blameless." No truly Christian heart can well be insensible to appeals like these. 'The Master comes. He comes to pass judgment upon your work. He comes to conduct you to the new heavens and new earth, where you are to dwell with him forever. Therefore, prepare to meet Him.'

We are not without examples to show the effect of this where it is really believed. Instances are constantly occurring of Christians who are stricken by some incurable malady, and compelled to believe that 'The Lord is at hand.' And from the moment this conviction is established in their minds, all other interests give place to their preparation for his advent. His word is their companion. His precious promises are their support. They are earnest in examining the foundations of their hope. They are most anxious that their repentance should be deep and sincere. They are 'sober.' They 'watch unto prayer.' They gird their loins and trim their lamps. They 'lay aside every weight and the sin which doth so easily beset them,' and patiently await his coming—'looking unto Jesus.'

We have all seen this. It must needs be so with a believer who knows that 'The Lord is at hand.' And were this sentiment wrought into the heart of the Church as it ought to be, it would yield the same fruit with all his followers. Nor is it of any force to reply, that the case of a Christian anticipating death is widely different from that of other Christians. The several passages quoted from the sacred oracles, the text itself included, were addressed, not to the dying, but to the living—to those who were engaged in all the activities of life, and who might perhaps anticipate length of days with as much reason as any of us. It is to these the Saviour and his apostles say, 'The Lord is at hand.' 'The judge standeth before the door.' 'I will come again and receive you unto myself.' For they, like all other men, ourselves among them, were liable to die at any moment. And it was the part of prudence, therefore, and of Christian duty, to be habitually mindful of this. It may be true of some of us, with a certainty which does not even appertain to individuals who *appear* to be drawing nigh to the grave, that 'The Lord is at hand.' And the point I am enforcing is, that if we felt this as we should feel it, it would be a great antidote to the torpor and the lassitude of our personal Christianity. We should be more concerned to make our calling and election sure. We should struggle more manfully against our besetting sins. It would put us upon a more thorough searching of our own hearts, that every lawless passion might be subdued, that every impure motive might be discarded, that every unholy desire might be detected and crucified. It would supply the defects and smooth down the excesses which deform the characters of so many Christians. It would repress those mischievous tempers which alienate brethren, and sow discord in the household of faith. It would admonish every Diotrephes against loving to have the pre-eminence, and every Demas against the love of this present world, and every Archippus against the neglect of his ministry, and every pains-taking Martha against being cumbered with much serving.

Every Christian, indeed, would feel the beneficial effect of this general conviction, that 'The Lord is at hand.' The entire Christianity of the Church would develop itself, if not in new forms, at least with an energy and a beauty now presented only in exceptional cases, which deserve, as they receive, the encomiums of all who can appreciate genuine piety. For, humbling as the confession is, it must be made, that the sentiment we are inculcating has but a languid hold upon the mass even of real believers, and that the spectacle is rarely witnessed even of a single Church whose whole organic life is animated by this principle. What we all need is a stronger faith,—a more implicit belief in the verities of God's word; and especially a profounder sense of that most pregnant truth, 'The Lord is at hand.' This would, by God's blessing, lift our Christianity out of the dust, and gird it with strength, and clothe it with beauty, and disencumber it of the misgivings and the falterings, the selfishness and the worldliness with which it is now clogged, and so make it less unworthy of that sacred name into which it has been baptized.

To be more specific:—a decisive effect would be produced, so it is reasonable to presume, upon the spirituality of the Church, and the maxims by which it is governed in the *training of its children* and the *administration of its stewardship*. How closely the Church had approximated to the world, and how much it needed that great revival of interest in Christian truth with which it has pleased God to visit our land, must be too well known to require illustration. Of the several points of delinquency which pertained to this wide-spread declension, there was none more conspicuous, none more affecting, than the withholding of the children of the covenant from Him to whom they had been solemnly dedicated. The seal of the covenant was upon them, but that was all. They were trained for the world. And as they grew up the world claimed and received its own.

So, also, it was to a large extent with the *wealth* of the Church. Ostensibly consecrated to God, his treasury was put off with a pittance; and the rest was appropriated to luxury, or handed over to indefinite accumulation.

I am speaking in the past tense. If these things are still so, there can be no better corrective for them than the one supplied by our text. I do not say, for I do not believe, that the conviction that 'The Lord is at hand' will, of itself, relax the grasp of avarice and open its coffers to the poor. If there be any office in the routine of human affairs which demands the right of Omnipotence, it is that of making a penurious man liberal. But the covetousness of the Church, the parsimony which contrives to live and even flourish, where, in the judgment of charity, there is a spark of true religion, this may be reached by the conviction of the approach of the Lord. The more vividly this sentiment is impressed upon the conscience of the Church, the more thoroughly will she be purged of that cupidity which is an opprobrium to her name, and a crime against Him, who, though rich, for her sake became poor, that she through his poverty might be rich.

And whenever, under the influence of this feeling, the Church surrenders her silver and gold to her Redeemer, she will no longer refuse him her children. Let it be once consciously felt that 'The Lord is at hand,' and the very parents who have sold their children to the world for a mess of pottage, will hasten after them to reclaim them, if it may be, and bring them to Jesus of Nazareth.

Fearful will be our final account, if we have been faithless to this trust. Let the announcement that 'The Lord is at hand' stir us all up to greater earnestness and prayer in seeking the salvation of our children.

. It seems to have been with some reference to the *wrongs* to which they were exposed, and the perils of their situation, that the Apostle reminded the Philippians of the approach of their Lord. "Let your moderation be known unto all men. The Lord is at hand. Be careful for nothing; but in everything by prayer and supplication with thanksgiving let your request be made known unto God." The word translated 'moderation' has no equivalent in our language. It seems to denote here a certain sweetness and serenity of temper, which takes all things in good part, and is not disturbed even by casualties and injuries. Whether we connect the text, then, with this clause, or with the exhortation which follows, there is a friendly remonstrance here against excessive anxiety or resentment when exposed to misfortunes or suffering injustice. A rare achievement it is to be able to suffer thus. Some of the strongest passions of our nature rebel against it. Nay, we are ruffled not merely on great occasions, but by the most insignificant occurrences. We allow the veriest trifles to disturb our equanimity, and enkindle our angry feelings. The Scripture remedy for this is, 'The Lord is at hand.' A mind suitably impressed with this truth will not be thrown from its balance by any of the minor troubles of life. You cannot realize that your Saviour is near, and that you may hear his summons at any moment, without knowing that He will redress your wrongs. Rather will you say with the Psalmist, ' The

Lord is on my side; I will not fear: what can man do unto me?' And should you even be assailed by malevolent calumnies, or despoiled of your property, it will still soothe you to remember that 'The Lord is at hand.'

What this conviction will do for the injured, it will as certainly do for the *afflicted*. And in this view, there must be those here who will have occasion for it. We know not how or where trouble may come; but this year would be unlike all the years which have preceded it, if it should fail to bring its cup of sorrow to some of our households. Whenever that occurs, it may be a solace to reflect that 'The Lord is at hand.' At hand he will be in the sense of that gracious promise, 'When thou passest through the waters, I will be with thee.' This thought is always a cordial to the afflicted believer. If sorrow be an essential part of his heritage, he knows that it neither comes unsent, nor without the presence of One who can be touched with a feeling of his infirmities. Nor need he turn away from the other aspect of this averment. To one who is deeply afflicted, it is a consolation to know that these trials must have an end; that He who in love and faithfulness sends them, if not already at the door, is still not far away, and will, in his own time and way, come and receive his stricken ones to himself, and conduct them to a world where God himself shall wipe away all tears from their eyes. Let mourners think of this. Let the infirm and the sick think of it. Let the unfortunate, who are perpetually struggling with calamities and disappointments, think of it. Let those who have to contend with the bitter trials of poverty, think of it. Let the parents who have nourished and brought up children, only to have unfilial hands plant their pillows with thorns, think of it. 'The Lord is at hand.' Your trials will soon be at an end. And then shall you go to be for ever with your Lord.

But there is still another form of trouble which has its balm and medicine here. It is that which made the apostle cry, 'Oh, wretched man that I am; who shall deliver me from the body of this death!' No Christian here can be a stranger to it,—this ceaseless warfare with sin and temptation. It pertains to the daily life of his soul. Sometimes it rages with a violence which threatens to uproot all the foundations of his hope, and to reimpose the vile fetters from which he was once emancipated. So profound is the subtlety of sin, so malevolent its spirit, so insatiable its cravings, so various its resources, so indomitable its energies, so skilful its devices, that it succeeds too often in ensnaring even the holiest men. And there are periods, perhaps, in the experience of most Christians when "the proud waters" so go over their souls, and their bosoms become such a very chaos of anxious, desponding, tumultuous feelings, that they can but fall prostrate before God, and cry—

> "Thou Infinite in love,
>   Guide this bewilder'd mind
> Which, like the trembling dove,
>   No resting-place can find
> On the wild waters; God of light,
> Thro' the thick darkness, lead me right!
>
> Bid the fierce conflict cease,
>   And fear and anguish fly;
> Let there again be peace,
>   As in the days gone by:
> In Jesus' name I cry to Thee,
> Remembering Gethsemane."

These are seasons for the Christian to welcome the announcement, 'The Lord is at hand!' His earthly ties may be strong and tender, and his position one which awakens the envy of his fellows. But they see only the surface. There are—

'Sins and doubts, and fears'

within that seemingly tranquil breast, which would sometimes make life insupportable, were it not for the promised coming of the Great Deliverer, and the pledge of an eternal discharge from this warfare. He fights on therefore, for he knows that the Captain of his salvation is near, and that the struggle cannot last always.

Think of this, my brethren, in the conflicts which indwelling sin and the arch-adversary are preparing for you. Remember that the battle is not yours, but God's, and that God, though invisible, is at hand, and will never leave you to fall a prey to your adversaries. Only 'be faithful unto death, and He will give you a crown of life.'

There are many other topics which would properly fall to be considered under this text; but I must not detain you. Let me not, however, dismiss the subject without again exhorting you all to bring home this scripture to your hearts and cherish it day by day, *as a stimulus to personal duty.*

Without recurring to duties already specified, let me remind every Christian here of the work he has to do for the unconverted around him. You know their condition—'without God and having no hope in the world.' Ponder well the fact, that 'The Lord is at hand;' and then decide what you will do for them. Peradventure his coming may be no blessing to *you*, should he find you a hinderance instead of help to the salvation of your fellow-sinners.

And there is that in this reflection which might seem enough to put you, my impenitent friends, upon the most resolute efforts to secure the forgiveness of your sins. 'The Lord is at hand!' As yet, He is near you in mercy—waiting to be gracious to you. But it cannot always be thus. His patience has a limit. His long-suffering may be exhausted. And then, 'what shall *the end* be of them that obey not the Gospel of God?'

Happy will it be for you, should you enter upon this year under the full influence of the feeling, that 'THE LORD IS AT HAND.' For, thus, you would begin to *live*. And surely it is time. Years enough have been given to sin and folly. Years enough have gone with their dark calendar of unpardoned offences to meet you at the bar of Christ. Let *this* year be dedicated to God. Let this primal Sabbath of the year mark the great epoch of your existence, when, by the help of God, you resolved to renounce the world and give yourselves to the Saviour in an everlasting covenant.

1860.

III.

"I WILL REJOICE IN THE LORD."

HABAKKUK III. 18.

Such is the text of Holy Scripture which I have to propose to you as your motto for the year. The beautiful passage in which it occurs will be noticed hereafter. For the rest, indulge me in that familiar style of address which I feel to be more appropriate to the occasion than an elaborate discourse.

The announcement will fall upon some incredulous ears, but is nevertheless true, that our religion is a *religion of joy*. This might be anticipated from the character of the Deity. As a Being of infinite goodness, He must delight in the happiness of his creatures. The glimpses we have of heaven exhibit that glorious realm to us as the scene of perfect and universal joy. The same benevolence which confers this affluence of bliss upon the angels would impress itself upon any system of relief designed for our world. That this has been done—only in a far higher degree than it was ever experienced or needed by the angels—is demonstrated by a single glance at the cross. With the *cross* in view, nothing in the way of love and pity can astonish us. 'He that spared not his own Son, but delivered him up for us all, how shall He not with him also freely give us all things?' It is impossible that a religion which is founded upon the incarnation and death of the Son of God should not be adapted to make men happy here and hereafter. We find, accordingly, that joy has been one of the characteristics of the Church under all dispensations. It was made a specific duty of the Hebrews to 'rejoice before the Lord' for days together in certain of their festivals. It is the constant strain of prophets and apostles,—'Rejoice in the Lord, O ye righteous.' The Church, speaking by the mouth of Isaiah, says, 'I will greatly rejoice in the Lord;' and Joel, "Ye children of Zion, rejoice in the Lord;" and Zechariah, 'Their heart shall rejoice in the Lord;' and Paul, 'Rejoice in the Lord alway: and again I say, rejoice.'

The primitive Christians understood this. They presented to an astonished world the spectacle of a joyful religion in circumstances which, by any earthly standard, might have seemed sufficient to hold them in terror and despondency all the while. From witnessing their Lord's ascension, they 'returned to Jerusalem with great joy, and were continually in the temple, praising and blessing God.' After the day of Pentecost, they continued daily in the temple, eating their meat with gladness and singleness of heart. When arraigned before the Council for preaching Christ, they departed 'rejoicing that they were counted worthy to suffer shame for his name.' Paul and Silas prayed and sang praises to God at night in the prison at Philippi. And we learn from one of the Epistles of St. Peter that the dispersed Christians to whom he wrote, rejoiced in Christ 'with joy unspeakable and full of glory.'

Such was the Christianity of the apostolic age. Such ought to be the Christianity of every age. If the religion of our day be deficient in this divine element, it is the more becoming that we should take the sentiment with us along the unknown paths of this opening year, 'I will rejoice in the Lord.'

'*In the Lord*'—you will observe. It is not every kind of joy that will answer either to the teachings of Scripture, or to our necessities. There must be many who are saying to themselves to-day, 'This year shall be to me a joyful year. I mean to seek my fill of pleasure wherever it is to be found. What is life without joy?' You are right—'What is life without joy?' But are you certain that what you call 'joy' is the reality or a counterfeit? I will not dispute its reality—*while it lasts;* still less challenge its fascinations. But will it bear the test of a thorough scrutiny? Can you find place for it when you take a comprehensive survey of life, and look to the end of things as well as to the beginning thereof? It is conjectured that Solomon wrote the book of Ecclesiastes in his old age to record his own experience of the sins and follies of the world. In the first part of the book he describes the careful and costly experiment he made—too costly and magnificent except for a powerful monarch—to frame to himself a scene of true enjoyment out of merely earthly materials. And no sooner does he present to our eyes the lofty and gorgeous fabric, than he writes upon it in blazing capitals, 'Vanity of vanities, all is vanity.' With not less significance does he afterward address the young in this strain:—'Rejoice, O young man, in thy youth; and let thy heart cheer thee in the days of thy youth, and walk in the ways of thine heart, and in the sight of thine eyes: but know thou that for all these things God will bring thee into judgment.'

Say not that this casts a deep shadow over life. There is not one ingredient in this teaching of the Bible on this subject, which is unfavorable to your present enjoyment. It simply requires that you seek that kind of enjoyment which will be satisfying and permanent. And in very kindness it warns you of what you must unavoidably learn in the end, that the joy *you* have in view is evanescent and illusive.

The joy of which the prophet speaks in the text, and which is intended in the other passages just quoted, springs from *faith in Christ*. "In whom *believing*, ye rejoice." The truths of Scripture can effect us only as they are believed. The stronger our faith, the more they must influence us. It is the property of faith to give a present reality to the objects and interests of the invisible world. It is the *substance* of things hoped for, the *evidence* of things not seen. A faith absolutely perfect would take the same hold upon the 'things not seen,' which our senses do upon the material things around us. It would, therefore, raise its possessor above the world. It would prevent him from over-valuing the objects which are most prized among men, and from sinking under trials. He would see everything here as in the light of eternity. And he would draw peace and comfort from sources which lie infinitely beyond the reach of any unbeliever.

A moment's reflection must suffice to show that every true Christian has the most ample warrant for saying, 'I will rejoice in the Lord.' For the entire body of revealed truth, all its doctrines, precepts, and promises, rightly apprehended, must be a fountain of joy to him. Not to dwell upon the character and perfections of Jehovah, who is the source and spring of all the goodness and all the happiness in the universe, consider the work of Redemption. This theme is so familiar that we speak of it with little or no emotion. But what would have been our condition without it? Suppose no purpose of mercy towards our species had been formed in the councils of the Godhead. Suppose Christ Jesus had not come into the world to save sinners. Suppose there had been no atonement, no mission of the Spirit, no Bible, no Church, no Sabbath. Every one sees what must have ensued with us. Or, if there be any who do not see, let them look at the fallen angels and they will see. Must it not, then, be a reason for joy that the reverse of all this has taken place?

Just in proportion as your faith may enable you to estimate the evils involved in the loss of the soul, and the blessings involved in its salvation, must you 'rejoice in the Lord.' It is not for a careless man to understand this. But you, my brethren, know what it is to be 'convinced of sin.' You have felt the terrors of an awakened conscience. You have felt yourselves exposed to the wrath of God. And you know something of the joy described by the Psalmist, 'Blessed is he whose transgression is forgiven, whose sin is covered. Blessed is the man unto whom the Lord imputeth not iniquity, and in whose spirit there is no guile.'

And what a privilege is it to have such a Saviour—one who unites in himself the divine and human natures, whose tenderness is commensurate with his majesty, and whose arms offer an unfailing sanctuary to needy and guilty sinners.

Not less comforting is the doctrine of the Holy Spirit, —his ministry of mercy to the Church, his perpetual abiding there, and his inexhaustible love and compassion to his people.

Then come the 'great and precious promises'—with balm for every wound, and succor for every peril, and strength for every trial, to which the Christian is exposed in his mortal pilgrimage.

Nor may we omit the Scripture view of Providence. It can be no trivial consolation to the believer, that it is his own God and Saviour who is on the throne; that He upholds, directs, and governs all things; and that under his beneficent administration all the Divine dispensations towards him shall work together for his ultimate good.

And then, to crown all, there is heaven itself,—that 'rest which remaineth unto the people of God,' and to which every real disciple has received a title—

'Purchased and sealed with blood Divine.'

Now the most indifferent person will admit that here are perennial springs of joy sufficient to meet all the cravings of the soul, and that, judged by its infallible text-book, Christianity may well claim to be a joyful religion. Yet the counter-admission must be made on our part, that it does not always present this aspect to the world. Its disciples do not habitually 'rejoice in the Lord,' as the primitive believers did. We must even concede that there is a type of religion prevalent amongst us which is seriously deficient in this element of joyfulness, or, at least, in the manifestation of it. Without stopping to seek a full explanation of this phenomenon, it may be suggested, that if there were more religion it would display itself more distinctly in all its proper characteristics. Allowing for exceptional cases, those Christians who are marked by a consistent and growing piety are usually very happy in their religion. It should not excite surprise that a piety which is sickly and precarious yields its possessor no joy.

Again, joy, as we have seen, is the fruit of faith. Faith has respect to the teachings of Scripture. A strong faith follows the patient and prayerful study of the Bible. It implies a clear apprehension of its cardinal doctrines. This cannot be claimed as a special characteristic of the Christianity of our times. It is a Christianity which has more length and breadth than depth. It is diffused and diffusive, but it does not always feed upon 'the strong meat of the word.' Where it does this, it is not lacking in joy. For it is impossible to meditate with an intelligent and appropriating faith upon those sublime and blessed truths which lie at the basis of the Gospel without 'rejoicing in the Lord.'

And is it an error to intimate that we are too much trained to regard doubts and misgivings as a *necessary part* of religion? There is very little of this, perhaps none at all, to be detected in the portraitures of the believers sketched in the book of Acts. The Christians of the next two centuries were equally remarkable for their exemption from it. Their simple faith took God at his word; and when once led to Christ they were not afraid to trust in him and to take the comfort of it. It is the reproach of our Christianity that there should be so few who can say, 'I *know* whom I have believed.' Where this can be said, there is joy of course.

But without enlarging on these points, let me rather commend to you the duty and privilege of rejoicing in the Lord. God requires this at your hands. "A faith without joy, is an altar without perfumes. Joy is the token and the ornament of gratitude. Joy should crown all our feelings towards God, and all our acts of religion. Even when we fast, we should anoint our head and wash our face. Will any one pretend that God discerns, in the human multitude, his own redeemed ones by the paleness of the countenance and the gloomy expression of the eyes? And would not the hymn of gladness among the angels in heaven over the conversion of a sinner, which makes them rejoice more than the perseverance of ninety and nine believers,—would not that hymn cease were the sinner himself not to rejoice over his own salvation? It is our joy, and not our sadness, that can do honor to God."*

This is further commended to us by the reflection, that rejoicing in God is an important *means of spiritual strength and progress.* It was no figure of speech which Nehemiah used when he kindly reproved the weeping of the people, and said to them, 'The joy of the Lord is your strength.' Joy is always an element of strength. You see it in every walk of life. A joyous spirit is a well-spring of energy, even though it have no connection with religion. Look at the merchant who carries it into the details of a complex and extended business; at the

* Vinet.

mechanic who carries it into his daily toil; at the traveller who cheers himself with it as he crosses mountains and deserts. How much a joyous spirit lightens their burdens and gives elasticity to their steps! It is the same in social life. This temper is very apt to indicate energy of character,—not, necessarily, energy directed by the highest wisdom, but still a capacity for exertion which is sure to bring something to pass.

If this be so with natural joy, the 'joy of the Lord' cannot be a less efficient principle. Nothing drinks up the spirits like a sense of God's displeasure. It is a palsy to all the powers of the soul. But the sense of his love invigorates every faculty and stimulates to the highest exertion. That is a striking passage in the fifty-first Psalm, as true to philosophy as it is to religious experience:—" Restore unto me the joy of thy salvation; and uphold me with thy free spirit. Then will I teach transgressors thy ways, and sinners shall be converted unto thee." His consciousness of guilt overwhelmed him. He lay prostrate in the dust. But if it should please God to speak peace to his conscience and restore the joy he had lost, *then* he would resume his neglected labors for the salvation of sinners, and they would be converted unto God. So it is with all Christians. When your hope of heaven is clear and undoubted, and you are rejoicing in the Lord, you serve him with alacrity. You are ready for any work to which he may appoint you. You go about it, not as a task, but as a privilege. If you are cheered by the sympathy of your fellow-Christians, well and good. But this is not your main reliance. There is a spring of activity within which would impel you onward even if there were no human eye to see, and no earthly tongue to applaud, your labors.

This is a great truth we are dealing with. The constant inquiry is, How can we make Christianity more effective in its warfare with sin and error? Let Christians "rejoice in the Lord;" and the problem is resolved. Properly regarded, his service demands this spirit. It is not a bondage, but perfect freedom. 'My yoke is easy, and my burden is light.' The Saviour has made full provision for the protection and comfort of all who engage in his service, without requiring them to wait for their crowns of glory. Just in proportion as they imbibe the true spirit of discipleship, will their work yield them genuine satisfaction; and this, in turn, will augment their capacity for useful effort. Among the crowd of active Christians who adorn our churches there are very many who do "rejoice in the Lord." And this not only increases their strength, but makes them welcome in many a circle where, if they were of a morose or moping spirit, the door would be closed against them.

This suggests as another reason for cultivating this temper, that *we owe it to the world.* Our Saviour has said, "Ye are the salt of the earth." "Ye are the light of the world." We have no right to give the world a mistaken idea of religion. They are more apt to form their conceptions of it from the characters and conduct of professing Christians than from the Bible. And when we so carry ourselves as to produce the impression that Christianity is all gloom, we do both them and religion a serious wrong.

There is, to be sure, a vicious mode of guarding against this error, viz., by following the world into its gaieties. You mean by doing this to show that religion is no patron of asceticism. But what right have you to pretend, especially in dealing with the unconverted, that religion *is* the patron of their frivolous amusements? To rejoice in their forbidden pleasures, is a very different thing from rejoicing in the Lord. Each necessarily excludes the other. The one is a sin; the other is a duty. If you mean to help the world, you must perform the duty, not practise the sin. It is no real help to them to show them that religion will let you go wherever they go, and do whatever they do. For if this be so, why should they change? What they need is, to be assured that religion has joys which are as superior, as they are unlike, to theirs. Show them that it has made you happier than you ever were before, and that without being indebted to their pleasures. Do this, and you will be helping them.

You will not infer from this that the Christian must sever himself from all worldly enjoyments. Far from it. Christian joy is not thus exacting. "Heavenly in its nature, it blends with terrestrial joys without losing aught of its purity, and without taking from them aught of their artless simplicity. The Christian, just before he is nearest to heaven, knows best how this world is to be enjoyed. The enjoyments of nature, of art, of society, appear to have trusted him with their most profound secret. The more his joy is serious and calm, the greater the certainty it is true. The more it is envied, the greater desire will be felt to ascertain its source. Thus, the Christian's happiness makes converts to the Gospel." But he can make no converts by participating in those pleasures which are forbidden him. The fatal tendency of this is, to wed the careless to their idols, and hurry them on to ruin.

It were easy to multiply arguments on this point. They will be implied, if not stated, in what I have further to say by way of commending the text to you as your motto for the year. A twelve-month since it was proposed to you as your talisman, 'The Lord is at hand!'. This has proved a prophetic announcement with some who were with us then. The rest of us are spared to stand upon the threshold of a New Year. Like each one that has preceded it, the year comes with its mercies and trials, its smiles and its frowns. It will bring unlooked-for blessings, and unexpected sorrows. No one amongst us may presume to forecast the specific changes it has in store for him. But the text may serve, by God's blessing, to prepare us for whatever He is preparing for us, and to enter upon a new period with the feeling, 'I will rejoice in the Lord.'

This resolution may be commended to those who seem least to require it—the *prosperous*. No doubt you are accustomed to rejoice. But it is rejoicing *in God* which he requires of you. And surely he has a right to require it. How is it that you are rich, while others are poor? That health reigns in your household, while others are smitten with disease? That the hours which come to so many surcharged with sorrow, come to you freighted with mercies? The Giver of all good is making this appeal to your gratitude. Do not rest in his gifts; but look through them to their Author. If you rejoice in them, as you may and should, yet rejoice chiefly in Him. For if such are the streams, what must the Fountain be? Then only can you derive the full measure of enjoyment from them, when you receive them as the fruits of his bounty, and love and serve Him with a grateful heart.

There is a sad ingratitude and selfishness which follows too often in the train of prosperity. The daily incense goes up from more cottages than palaces. The crust of bread elicits a hymn of praise; the table groaning under its costly viands becomes a daily holocaust to appetite and pride. Men are not content unless they can banish God from their pleasures. Willing enough to accept his gifts, they seem to feel that in so far as they have to acknowledge him, it is to that extent a practical deduction from the true enjoyment of life. Strange they should not consider that no form or scene of happiness can be lasting, which excludes Him from whom alone all happiness flows.

This, indeed, is an urgent reason why you should adopt the maxim, 'I will rejoice in the Lord.' Now you have other means of enjoyment. But you may not have them long. This very year may see you stripped of your property. Or it may see your family broken and shattered by death. Or, worse than poverty or death, it may see some of your blessings turned into implements of torture which will embitter your days. What you need, what every one needs, is a portion which is exposed to none of these casualties; a joy which, being not of earth, nothing earthly can take from you. And this you will have only when you can say, 'I will rejoice in the Lord.'

But you will all feel that the real difficulty lies in another direction. 'It is well enough,' you are ready to say, 'to bid the prosperous rejoice, but is it not a mockery to address this exhortation to the *sorrowful?*'

To those who know of no joy but that of the world, it must seem a mockery. But Christian joy is a different emotion—different in its source, different in its aliment, different in its expression. To invite the sorrowful to join in any demonstration of boisterous mirth, or even to be present at ordinary scenes of festivity, would be rude and insulting. But the joy which enters into the believer's heritage is a hidden principle lodged in the depths of the heart by the Divine Spirit, and nourished there by his own Almighty hand. It does not imply—for that is not its nature—a state of constant excitement, an effervescence and transport of the animal feelings. This is the familiar idea of joy among the votaries of worldly pleasure. But religious joy is something deep, pure, calm, abiding; not without its ebbs and flows, its raptures and depressions, but, on the whole, tranquil and serious,—'a holy joy,' as it is well expressed.

This being its nature, there is no incongruity in calling even upon those Christians who have much cause for sadness to adopt the resolution, 'I will rejoice in the Lord.' In one aspect, this may be affirmed of Christians generally. For the whole Christian life is a struggle with sin, and sin must needs bring sorrow in its train. But this conflict does not necessarily extinguish the believer's joy. The sacred flame may continue to glow upon his altar, though exposed to the beating storm of adversity and the fiercer blasts of his own passions. No Christian was ever placed in circumstances to test this more thoroughly than the great apostle of the Gentiles. It was the high privilege conferred upon him—he treats it as a privilege—that he was appointed to endure a greater variety and amount of suffering for his Master, than almost any other of whom we read. There are touching allusions in his epistles which show that he was no Stoic under these trials. It is apparent that he was not a stranger to despondency. But in the main, the whole tone of his writings, like the whole tenor of his life, is that of an eminently happy and joyful man. It is one of the series of paradoxes in which he has summed up his own Christian life, 'as sorrowful, yet *always rejoicing.*' It is scarcely possible to think of him, whether preaching to a popular assembly, or pleading before kings; whether hastening from city to city with the everlasting Gospel, or shut up in a dungeon; whether sitting in council with the apostolic college, or comforting his companions amidst the horrors of a shipwreck; except as a man imbued with a heavenly serenity and joy, the fitting counterpart of his lofty intrepidity and heroism.

Nor was this any prerogative of the apostleship. It is for other Christians also to say—thousands of them have said it—'As sorrowful, yet always rejoicing.'

I am not counselling you to attempt an impossibility. Still less am I inculcating an insensibility to trials. He who sends these trials means that they shall be felt. It is his own injunction, 'Hear ye the rod, and who hath appointed it.' But He designs, no less, that his people shall trust in him, and rejoice in him. Trouble is one of the messengers He sends to recall them to him :—" In their affliction, they will seek me early." To rejoice in Him at *such* a time—when the heart is pierced with sorrow, and his irresistible Providence is veiled in clouds and darkness—is one of the noblest tributes which can be paid to his wisdom and faithfulness. And why should it not be so? Viewed from that elevation to which a vigorous faith exalts the soul, these trials and temptations are all transitory. They cannot disturb the Christian's portion, nor invalidate his title to it. It still remains true that he has an Almighty Saviour; that the blessings of the unchangeable covenant are his; and that there is a crown of glory awaiting him. Let him, then, *rejoice in the Lord.*

This counsel is equally suited to occasions of public calamity and to those of private sorrow. It was with a prime reference to these the prophet used the words. The passage is too beautiful not to be familiar to every reader of the Bible. 'Although the fig-tree shall not blossom, neither shall fruit be in the vines; the labour of the olive shall fail, and the fields shall yield no meat; the flock shall be cut off from the fold, and there shall be no herd in the stalls; yet I will rejoice in the Lord, I will joy in the God of my salvation.' It may be that we shall have sad occasion for this scripture in its bearing upon *Divine judgments* before this year closes. What may be in reserve for our beloved country we know not. The omens at present are threatening enough to drive every Christian to the throne of grace; for that is the source whence help must come, if it comes at all. But whatever may happen, the believer has his resource:— 'I will rejoice in the Lord.'

This, then, is the temper with which it befits us to enter upon the opening year, and this the spirit we should strive to carry into all its engagements and businesses, all its sorrows and pleasures:—'I will rejoice in the Lord.' It will be our wisdom and duty to cherish more and more the conviction that we must seek our happiness in God. Let us acknowledge Him more in our plans. Let us remember Him in our ordinary occupations, in our social recreations, and in our hours of solitude. Let it be the habit of our lives to trust in Him, to seek his favor as the chiefest of blessings, and to rejoice in Him as 'the God of our salvation.' Could we but enter upon the year with this equipment of celestial temper, it would come to us richly freighted with joy, and the pleasant greeting of "A happy New Year," would have a fulness of meaning which we rarely attach to it.

Need I say how sincerely I pray that you may all experience its power and preciousness? *All* of you! It is one of the painful reflections of this hour, that there are those here who have never even begun to 'Rejoice in the Lord;'—to whom, indeed, the very phrase may be unmeaning, if it is not positively disagreeable. Alas, my dear people, to what end are you living? What record have your past years borne to the bar of God? And of what value is all the 'happiness' you have, up to this time, garnered from the world? Is it too much to believe that there must be those among you who are dissatisfied with themselves and with the illusive joys they have hitherto pursued? Is it too much to hope that there may be some who would fain begin a New Year with a new life? Let me entreat you not to stifle the secret longing. It may be the still, small voice of the Spirit inviting you to the skies. It is a period which inclines us to reflection—this shadowy line between the Old Year and the New. And here, as you are framing your plans, give place at length to God and Redemption. Aspire to something higher and nobler than these earth-born joys. Put away the sins which have so long separated you from God and from happiness. Come to the fountain which alone can cleanse you. And resolve in God's strength—'I WILL REJOICE IN THE LORD.' Thus shall you find rest unto your souls; and through the long cycles of eternity, this year shall be of blessed memory as the year of your espousals to Christ.

IV.

"THIS IS MY FRIEND."

SONG OF SOLOMON v. 16.

What better could I do on this New Year's Sabbath, than offer to you as your motto for the year this brief and beautiful statement from the Book of Canticles? It is the language of the Church, the Lamb's Bride, concerning the Bridegroom—her and our Lord:—"This is my beloved and this is my friend, O daughters of Jerusalem!" There is no believer here who may not make this language his own. An unspeakable privilege it is, to be allowed to use it. And doubtless before the year is over, some of us may have occasion to prize this privilege even more highly than we do now.

It were very commonplace to address you on the advantages and delights of friendship. But it can never be unwelcome to you to hear of that Friend who is here brought to our notice. Let me talk with you about Him, as friends are wont to talk about an absent friend—familiarly and freely.

Yet the use of this word *absent* must remind us that there is something very peculiar in his character; for He is never absent. It is one of the unavoidable trials of all earthly attachments, that they involve occasional separations. In innumerable cases these separations are very frequent or very protracted, and aggravated by the endless hazards to which life and health are exposed. When two friends—or, if you will, an affectionate family—are restored to each other, with the prospect of remaining together for a long while, it seems to make their happiness almost complete. But a final separation must come; and in all ordinary instances it is preceded by numerous temporary absences.

With Jesus of Nazareth this cannot occur. From this Friend you not only may not, but cannot sever yourself. A change of residence or of circumstances—a journey—a sickness—is of no moment. He is with his friends as much at one time, or in one place, as another:—always a Friend at hand.

Every one will perceive what this implies in respect to his *rank and nature*. There are various paths by which we may ascend to the same sublime truth. But it flows inevitably from the one point we are now considering, that Jesus Christ must be Omnipresent; and if Omnipresent, he cannot be a mere creature. There can be but One Being who is ever with us and with millions besides in this land, and in other lands, and all over the globe. So that in the Friend who is never absent from him, the Christian also has a friend who is able to take care of him in all possible circumstances.

If a person were called to traverse a country filled with anarchy and violence, there is nothing he would desire so much as the company of some one of such rank and authority as to insure him protection. Such a situation is but an inadequate type of our condition in this world. It is a world broken away from its allegiance. It is in arms not only against its Prince, but against all who attempt to serve him. Its resources are too vast, and its hostility is too malignant, to be successfully resisted even by the most resolute of the race, in their own strength. They who have no succor from without must inevitably succumb.

To state the case in other language:—our condition here is such as to warrant no hope of deliverance if we are left to ourselves. Take the very best of the race—those who have escaped from the servitude of sin, and made good progress in the Christian life—what can they do in a conflict like this? What with indwelling depravity, the enticements of the world, and the machinations of Satan, they would be vanquished as fatally as David and Peter were. They would find their chains re-imposed, and their captivity renewed with stronger bolts and bars than ever.

Thanks be to God, these dangers are provided for. The believer has a Friend to accompany him, who is able to defend him. That may be truly said of Him, which was impiously said of Simon the Sorcerer, 'This man is the great power of God.' This very phrase, indeed, is applied to Him by the Divine Spirit: "Christ, the power of God." And He himself challenges the distinction as his own, when he says, 'All power is given to me in heaven and in earth.'

How this lifts the Saviour up infinitely above all other friends! We are none of us without friends in whose affection we have entire confidence. We know that they love us with a sincerity and a devotion which are beyond suspicion. We feel assured that they would do anything in their power to help us in a time of trouble. But without disparaging their fidelity and kindness, we cannot forget that their capacity to relieve us in sorrow or danger is limited. When they have done their utmost, the weight still presses, and the heart still bleeds. But with Him who has 'all power' it is otherwise. He can go down into the depths and take the gauge of the trouble that is crushing us; and then say to the desponding soul in tones which must be heard, 'Trust in the Lord for ever; for in the Lord Jehovah is everlasting strength.' Nor does it matter from what quarter the trial may come. His prerogative extends alike over the worlds of matter and of mind; as well over 'foul spirits' as over the lawless passions of the heart. And the humblest Christian may confidently say of him, 'He is my refuge and my fortress: my God; in Him will I trust.'

Omnipotence and ubiquity, important as they are, are not the only qualities which commend to us our Heavenly Friend. It is one of that golden cluster of titles by which he was heralded seven centuries before his advent, 'He shall be called . . . *Counsellor.*' In our present condition we need as much a wise friend as a powerful one. And the one attribute is as often wanting as the other. A friend may be very sincere and faithful who is in no way remarkable for wisdom. Some of the truest friends come short here. They may be pleasant companions. Their sympathy may be grateful to us. They may have that very rare 'power of silence' which enables them to forbear repeating what is said to them. And yet as advisers, they are but broken reeds. From a natural debility of judgment, or simply through the blinding influence of their affections, they can give only such counsel as they suppose will fall in with the inclinations of their friend. You cannot distrust their love; but you may well say to them, what the apostle said to his faithful Philippians:—"This I pray, that your love may abound yet more and more in *knowledge* and in all *judgment.*"

But not so with the Friend the text extols. As he is the 'power of God,' so is he the 'wisdom of God.' His own language is, 'Counsel is mine, and sound wisdom; I am understanding; I have strength.' He knows everything. With an eye that sweeps through the universe, he sees at a glance all the agencies and influences which can affect his friends for good or ill. He perceives at once every plot which is contrived for their injury; every snare spread for their feet; every arm lifted to strike them. He is acquainted with the minutest incidents in the allotment of each one of them. There is no wrong they suffer, no danger they fear, no secret grief that preys upon their spirits, no burden whatever of sin or woe they bear, which is not known to him. And he knows, no less, just what to do for them. It may not be precisely what they would choose, but it is what they most need. Unlike an earthly friend, he is able to take in all the surroundings of the case; and to consider as well the ultimate result as the immediate effect of particular measures. And hence the deliverance or the strength he imparts, is uniformly designed to promote, if not the present ease, at least the future and permanent well-being of his people. For in him are hid all the treasures of wisdom and knowledge: and such a friend cannot but be the very "Counsellor" we require amidst the perplexities and conflicts of life.

This will be still more apparent, when it is considered, that He is a friend who loves his people *with a love 'passing knowledge.'*

The strength of Christ's affection for his people, is not a matter of conjecture. Nor does the proof of it lie mainly in his own protestations, convincing as those would be. It is embodied in acts, which challenge the wonder and adoration of the universe. The entire Bible is a revelation of his love to them. It originated in the essential benevolence of his nature, eternal ages before our sphere was created. Even then, in the distant prospect of man's fall, he engaged to ransom him, and his "delights were with the sons of men." In the fulness of time, this love assumed to itself a human form; and there was no depth of humiliation and of suffering to which it did not stoop in order to snatch its endangered objects from destruction. 'Greater love hath no man than this, that a man lay down his life for his friends.' And this proof has he given us of his love. Nay, he has gone beyond this, for "even while we were yet sinners [and enemies] did Christ die for us." Had he been simply a creature of angelic rank, this could not have failed to produce a profound impression upon all holy beings. But what tongue shall attempt to portray this event as the voluntary sacrifice of God's own Son— 'the Brightness of the Father's glory and the Express Image of his Person!' It is the exalted rank, the eternal Deity, of the Saviour, which invests the transaction with its sublime interest, and makes it so impossible to describe it.

The believer exclaims, 'This is my Friend:'—and he bids you roll back the ages until you antedate the course of time, and see the Second Person of the adorable Trinity entering into a covenant with the Father to redeem a rebellious race not yet summoned into being. Again he exclaims, '*This* is my Friend!'—and he takes you to the little village of Bethlehem, to that manger which presents to you the most wonderful sight the sun —or any one of the myriad-suns of the firmament—had ever shone upon, an infant child bearing the Name of names, "IMMANUEL," "GOD WITH US." He cries again, "This is my Friend!"—and he leads you to Calvary, and shows you that spectacle which made the sun "shut his glories in," convulsed the earth to its centre, and even stirred the slumbering dead. Once more he exclaims, 'This is my Friend!'—and he conducts you on the wings of faith up to the heaven of heavens, and points you to 'the Lamb in the midst of the throne,' the object of universal homage and gratitude.

> "The head that once was crowned with thorns,
>   Is crowned with glory now;
> A royal diadem adorns
>   The mighty victor's brow.
> The highest place that heaven affords,
>   Is his by sovereign right;
> The King of Kings, and Lord of Lords,
>   And Heaven's Eternal Light!"

Yes, *this* is the believer's Friend. And these are but successive demonstrations of the boundless love he bears to his people. From eternity his heart was with them. It was with them through all his pilgrimage of sorrow and suffering in our world. It is with them still in his glory; for he "ever liveth to make intercession for them," and he is "Head over all things to the Church." Well may the apostle say of this love, "it passeth knowledge."

It is another conspicuous attribute of our Divine Friend, that he is *full of tenderness and sympathy.*

There is many a sterling character which nevertheless lacks this pleasant embellishment. We have all had friends upon whose attachment we could place implicit reliance, who might not always have the gentlest way of showing it. It is one of the marvels which cluster around the Saviour's character, that it combines the grandeur and omnipotence of a God with more than a mother's tenderness. There is something extremely beautiful and touching in the imagery Christ employs in unfolding his commission. "The Spirit of the Lord God is upon me, because the Lord hath appointed me to preach good tidings unto the meek; he hath sent me to bind up the broken-hearted, to proclaim liberty to the captives, and the opening of the prison to them that are bound." These prophetic strains pass into history in the New Testament. He stands before us there, the friend of publicans and sinners. He opens his lips, and it is to utter in the ears of that proud and scornful age strange words like these:—"Blessed are the poor in spirit!" "Blessed are they that mourn!" "Blessed are the meek!" We fall into his train, and for three years we are living among the objects of pity—the poor, the sick, and the suffering, who flock around him for relief. Nor are they more ready to come, than he is to succor them. Whether it be a group of miserable lepers, or a blind man by the wayside, or a ruler of the synagogue interceding for a daughter, or a Syro-Phenician mother on the same anxious errand, his ear responds to every appeal, and his hand is stretched forth in its unwearied ministry of mercy. We claim, then, that he is a Friend no less remarkable for his tenderness and pity, than for his power and majesty.

To view our Lord in one more only of the many aspects of his friendship to his people, he is a *faithful* friend. He is faithful in that he will reprove the errors and sins of his people. This is one of the rarest qualities among friends; but to a true, ingenuous heart, one of the most valuable. "As an ear-ring of gold, and an ornament of fine gold, so is a wise reprover upon an obedient ear." The Saviour loves his friends too well to 'suffer sin upon them.' When they go astray, he will find means, by his Spirit, or through the voice of conscience, to say to them, 'I have not found thy works perfect before God.' 'Remember from whence thou art fallen, and repent, and do the first works.' He is *faithful*, again, in that he is not readily alienated by the misconduct of his people. See how he bore with the faults of his disciples. And where has been the disciple since who has not sometimes tested his long-suffering! Yet he does not cast off any. He exemplifies, rather, the lesson he inculcated on a certain occasion, "I say unto you, *forgive* until seventy times seven." And, again, he is *faithful* because, as this language implies, he is unchangeable. Whom he loves, he loves to the end. To every believer he says, "I have loved thee with an everlasting love,"—a protestation which carries heaven and eternal glory in its bosom.

Such are some of the attributes which meet in the character of Jesus of Nazareth,—*ubiquity, power, wisdom, love, tenderness, faithfulness*,—and all in an infinite degree. Thrice happy must he be who is able to say, "This is *my* FRIEND!" And this may be said by every sincere Christian here—the youngest equally with the oldest; as well the poorest as the richest.

In this friendship there is something very wonderful, if we do but allow ourselves to consider it. Other friendships usually include three conditions, not one of which is found here. These are, equality of rank, personal merit, and a capacity, to some extent, of reciprocating favors. But in this case, the parties are the Creator and the creature; the self-existent and supreme Jehovah and a worm of the dust. As to merit, there was everything in the character of man to repel affection. Not only was he destitute of that holiness in which alone a holy God could feel any complacency, but his attitude towards his Maker was that of a rebel and an enemy. And so far from being able to reciprocate kindnesses, his inevitable and constant condition was one of dependence and want. He could be only a recipient, never a giver. Still, the friendship was established. The ineffable wisdom and unquenchable love of the Redeemer, disregarding even obstacles so formidable as these, stooped to the necessities of our fallen nature, and exalted the miserable slaves of sin to the dignity and happiness of friends of God. Let us not forget, if we, any of us, share this high distinction, that it was purchased for us at an infinite cost. But it is time to make a personal application of the text.

In his address to the elders of the Church of Ephesus, the apostle said, " Behold, I go bound in the spirit unto Jerusalem, *not knowing the things that shall befall me there.*" We may each of us appropriate this language in respect to the year before us,— not knowing the things that shall befall me. This impenetrable curtain which hides the future from us, receding only as we press against it, and refusing us a glimpse even of the coming hour or the coming moment, is held in its place even more by the hand of love than by the hand of power. For whose life would not be shrouded in sorrow, if the future were unveiled to him! But while we know not what will happen, we know well what may happen; and this should be enough to consecrate in our affections the friendship we are commemorating.

Nothing, for example, is more probable than that occasions may arise during this year, which will bring with them *perplexing questions of duty.* Such questions are coming up in the ordinary routine of life—in the management of our families, and in the prosecution of business. They may come in graver aspect—questions which are to decide our future plans, or occupations, or homes. How easily we are confounded in emergencies of this sort, must be known to every one here. Our sagacity soon fails us, even when aided by the lights of experience. And we are not certain of faring any better, if we appeal to our friends. If we are able to say of Jesus Christ, "This is my Friend," there need be no disquietude. For "is anything too hard for *the Lord?*" It is no less your privilege than your duty to go to Him in every exigency. For "if any of you lack wisdom, let him ask of God, that giveth to all men liberally, and upbraideth not; and it shall be given him." To do this, there is no toilsome journey to be made, like that of the Queen of Sheba, when she went to see the glory of Solomon and to prove him with 'hard questions.' For, as we have seen, He is a Friend never absent. He can be consulted by any disciple at any moment. I do not say that we are authorized to expect an instant answer in some palpable form. All that we affirm, all that we can reasonably require, is, that, to the humble and importunate petition for direction He will ordinarily grant a gracious answer. By some impression upon the mind, or by some providential indications, a ray of light will fall upon the suppliant's path, which will at least relieve, if it does not remove, his embarrassment.

I speak of this habit of going to Christ with difficult questions, as not only a privilege but a duty. For we really have no right to choose our course without looking to Him. 'In all thy ways acknowledge Him.' Except we do this, we have no share in the promise annexed,— 'And he shall direct thy paths.' They who neglect to take counsel of their best Friend, must needs fall into many an error.

Again, it is quite certain that this year will be with every Christian here, a year of *conflict with sin;* and with some, peradventure, there may be experiences of *spiritual darkness and depression.* The Christian life involves conflict. It is in its very nature a war against sin. The contest varies with different persons in its concomitants; but while life lasts, 'the flesh lusteth against the spirit, and the spirit against the flesh.' Nor is it a struggle which any believer can wage successfully in his own strength. His foes are too many and too powerful for this. Armed with the subtlety and the malignity of sin, they are perpetually around his path. To fly from and to overcome them are alike impracticable. One resource alone he has, and it cannot fail him.

When chafed, and wearied, and wounded in this warfare, let him call to mind the saying that is written, 'This is my Friend.' Although this Friend has had no experience of indwelling sin, yet in every other respect, not only has He been 'tempted as we are,' but He has vanquished his and our enemies. The plenitude of the universe is at his disposal; and He is equally able and willing to sustain his people in their conflicts.

And especially will you need his help, should you be overtaken by days of darkness and despondency. For these are trials which not unfrequently bid defiance to human sympathy. The soul which is cast down under a dreadful sense of sin, or which is mourning the hidings of God's countenance, refuses to be comforted. Yet there is one resource which can avail you even in those unhappy circumstances. If you can but open your heart to the assurance, 'This is my Friend;' if you can but go to *Him* with your sorrows, you will find relief. For He came to 'bind up the broken-hearted.' And while his arm is mighty to save, the tenderness of his nature is a sufficient pledge that no 'bruised reed' will be refused his help.

The transition is natural from one class of trials to another. That there are sorrows on their way for some of us, which will overtake us before the year expires, may be safely taken for granted. In what form they are to come—loss of property, sickness, bereavement, death— or where they are to alight, He only knows, who knoweth all things. This, however, is certain. Whenever they come, and in whatever guise, nothing can so effectively disarm them of their terrors, as to be able to say, 'This is my Friend.' So the affrighted disciples found it, when their little bark was swept by the storm upon Genessareth. So Mary and Martha found it, when they mourned the death of their brother. So many a believer you have known and loved, has found it in sickness and in sorrow. The thought, 'This is my Friend,' has been like the balm of Gilead to their wounds, and nerved them to say, 'Not as I will, but as Thou wilt!'

For they well understand, that this trouble has not come without his permission—and that He is a friend too wise and too compassionate to have sent it unless it were for their good. They remember, too, that in assigning to them these painful experiences, He is but conducting them along the path which his own sufferings have sanctified. Their feeling is—

> "Christ leads me through no darker rooms
> Than He went through before;
> He that unto God's kingdom comes,
> Must enter by this door."

And they have the further conviction that He is always present with them, for, varying the figure, He 'sits like a refiner and purifier of silver,' watching the effect of the fire upon the precious metal, and ready to withdraw it as soon as it is sufficiently freed from its base alloy.

In reflections like these, you will find consolation under your trials. For what can we not endure, if we are only able to say, 'It is my Friend, who subjects me to this affliction. Yea, it is my best Friend. He has shown his love to me by dying for me. I cannot, will not, distrust Him even though He lead me by a path that I know not. For He knows what is for my good.

And I have his promise, As thy days, so shall thy strength be.'

The year, again, will bring its *duties*, no less than its trials:—and here it will be wholesome to recall our motto, 'This is my Friend.'

We have seen, though in a most imperfect and superficial way, what sort of a Friend He is; what sacrifices He has made, what blessings He has provided, for us. What more becoming than that we should daily ask ourselves the question, 'What am I doing—what can I do—to testify my gratitude to such a Friend?' If it were possible to secure the thorough and permanent lodgment of the feeling in every Christian heart here, 'This is my Friend,' this church would require little exhortation to duty during the present year. When applied to, as you so often are, for funds to aid in spreading the Gospel or relieving the destitute, your response would be, 'This is my Friend whose voice I hear: the silver and the gold are his, and I would not, if I might, withhold what is his own.' When summoned to engage in some work of Christian philanthropy, quite within the compass of your powers, though involving some self-denial, you would say again, 'It is my Friend who solicits my aid, and I cannot refuse Him, for He has said, Inasmuch as ye have done it unto one of the least of these my brethren, ye have done it unto me.' If again you should be admonished of the duty of attending faithfully upon the ordinances of the Sanctuary, on the Sabbath and during the week, you would be ready to say, 'It is my Friend who instituted these services. His presence hallows them, his glory shines through them, and He designed them for the nurture and comfort of my soul, and for the salvation of the perishing. I will not forsake the place where his honour dwelleth.' If solicited to give your countenance to some festivity, which your conscience whispers to you is forbidden ground to a follower of Jesus, your frank and manly reply would be, 'No, I could not approach my Friend and ask Him to go with me; I should but wound Him by going where I know He would not go; and it were base in me to purchase a transient gratification at the cost of grieving One who has shed his blood for me.'

And thus, all along the year will you find this text a ready help in resolving practical questions and carrying you up toward a loftier reach of Christian achievement. Amidst the endless variety of changes and circumstances which the year may bring with it, no situation can await you in which it will not be useful to you to think of Jesus of Nazareth with the feeling, 'This is my Friend.' Whenever this confidence animates the breast, and so long as it lasts, there are at least two things which will not be neglected.

One of these is *prayer*. Intercommunion is the soul of friendship. If we feel that Christ is our friend, we *must* desire to hold fellowship with Him. And this, in turn, cements the bond which unites us to Him.

The other is *an earnest desire and aim to make Christ known to others.* Unlike mere human friendships, there is no room for selfishness or jealousy here. On the contrary, the proper effect of being admitted to Christ's friendship is to enkindle the disposition to make others partakers of the same blessing. The more the heart glows under the radiance of the sweet conviction, 'This is my Friend,' the more irrepressible will be its longings to bring other friendless sinners to his feet.

Such, my brethren, is the text I tender to you as your maxim for the year. In your studies and in your business, in your journeys and in your recreations, in your joys and your sorrows, in your conflicts and your consolations, in the Church and in the world, in health and in sickness, in life and in death, it will strengthen, sustain, and sanctify you, to remember "This is my Friend."

Grateful as it is to utter words like these, they awaken one very sad reflection. I cannot but fear that there are some among my hearers who will not venture to appropriate this discourse to themselves. You shrink from saying, 'This is my Friend!' Alas for you, if all your friends are here in this world—frail, dying creatures, like yourselves. For, much as you may need a friend like Jesus now, you will need Him a thousandfold more when these other friends, and you with them, have passed into eternity. But why is He not your Friend? Is it his fault? Has He failed to tender you his friendship? Has He repelled you when you have gone to Him? Has He invited all others to trust in Him and share his love and confidence, and left you out? You will not say this. You have a monitor within which tells you that the blame of your being to-day without this Friend lies wholly at your own door. It is his own touching lament over you, 'Ye will not come unto me that ye might have life!' Oh, ye friendless souls, come to this Friend of sinners. Do not spend *another* year without Christ. But come to Him *now*. Begin this new year with a new life. Looking to the Almighty Spirit for grace to renew and guide you, humbly and penitently put your trust in the Redeemer. Then will you know the comfort bound up in those precious words, 'THIS IS MY FRIEND;' and the last great day shall see you owned of Him as *his* friend, in the presence of an assembled universe.'

1862.

V.

"FOR TO ME TO LIVE IS CHRIST."

PHILIPPIANS I. 21.

It may be safely said that the Bible itself contains nothing which would be more appropriate for the opening year than the text I have just given you. I may go further and add, that there is no greater blessing we could receive than to have these words indelibly engraved upon our hearts to-day by the Spirit of God, "To me to live is Christ." Could we all take this for our motto, and faithfully conform to it, it would make this year an epoch in our lives—a year to be remembered with gratitude through eternity. Let us see what it imports.

1. It imports that Christ *is the Source of the believer's life;* and that in a twofold sense.

The humbling representation of the Bible is, that our race is by nature spiritually dead. This does not mean that man has been deprived of any of his essential faculties; nor that he is incapable of exerting his powers for wise and noble purposes; nor that he may not on occasion display many admirable qualities. It means simply that he is destitute of holiness; that he has lost that which especially constituted the 'image of God' in which he was created; and that having become depraved in character, he has also drawn upon himself the penalty of the Divine law. He is dead inasmuch as his life is a forfeit to the justice of God; and he is dead inasmuch as sin has established its complete mastery over his soul.

This double death has been annulled by the interposition of Christ. It was his errand to our world, to 'destroy him that had the power of death,' and liberate his captives. This He effected by satisfying the claims of the law against them, in his 'obedience unto death;' and by sending the Holy Spirit to renew their hearts and unite them to Himself by a true faith.

Every Christian looks to Christ as the Procurer and Author of his life. He knows that but for his mediation, he must have remained for ever 'dead in trespasses and in sins.' And tracing back to his wondrous love the hopes which now animate his bosom, his habitual feeling is, "I live; yet not I, but Christ liveth in me; and the life which I now live in the flesh, I live by the faith of the Son of God who loved me and gave himself for me."

2. This implies that Christ is *the Preserver and Guardian* of the believer's life. We drop a seed into the ground, and go away with confidence that nature will do all the rest:—aided by the kindly warmth of the soil, the rains, and the sunshine, the germ will spring up and bear fruit, as a matter of course. Even here, however, there will be no fruit unless a pervading Providence give effect to these several agencies. And certainly in the spiritual world, while means are indispensable, means alone can accomplish nothing. The germ of life deposited in the renewed heart, unlike the seed you

plant in your garden, falls into a most ungenial soil. There is literally no nourishment for it there. All its surroundings are unfavorable. If it survives, it must survive not by reason of the elements which enfold it, but despite of them. It has its proper type, not in the flower in your garden, but in a taper thrown upon the sea. And yet it does live. The flame burns on; for it is fed by an unseen hand. "Your life is *hid with Christ* in God. When Christ *who is our life* shall appear,"— Here is the secret of what would otherwise be an inscrutable mystery—the conservation of this divine principle in the heart of the Christian. The remains of his own corrupt nature are all hostile to it. The whole course and current of the world's maxims and usages runs counter to it. It is exposed to the deadly assaults of Satan. And yet it lives. It lives because it has its vital origin in Christ. His omnipotence guards it. His hand nurtures it. When it is weak, He recruits it. When it has developed into the fruit-bearing plant, He takes his pruning-knife and 'purgeth it that it may bring forth more fruit.'

There is no experience of the believer more universal and decided than this of which I am speaking, namely, his constant and absolute dependence upon Christ for all that pertains to his new life. His necessities are not always the same; they vary with the endless diversities of character and condition which mark our earthly allotments. They vary as between different persons; and they vary with the changing circumstances of the same person. To-day we need wisdom; to-morrow it may be courage; anon it may be patience; and again strength; and so on indefinitely. The essential point is, that whatever the form or measures in which the spirit life needs to be reinforced, the required aid must come from one source. *In Christ* we 'have *all* and abound.' For 'in Him dwelleth all the fulness of the Godhead bodily;' and 'of his fulness have all we received.' On this ground do we affirm that Christ is the Preserver and Guardian of the believer's life.

3. Christ is *the End and Object* of the believer's life.

This, perhaps, is the thing chiefly intended by the avowal, 'To me to live is Christ.' It is as if St. Paul had said, "I have no other business, interest, honor, or pleasure, for which to live, but Christ and his glory, service, and favor. To know, to love, to follow Christ, is my life, my glory, my joy." To know what this protestation means from the lips of this great apostle, one must follow his radiant career for the thirty years which intervened between his memorable journey to Damascus and his martyrdom. From the day when the implements of persecution dropped from his hands at the feet of Jesus of Nazareth, until he sealed his devotion to Him with a martyr's death, the love of Christ glowed in his bosom with a pure and unquenchable ardor. It was his masterpassion, to which every other aim and sentiment paid homage. He could say "this *one thing* I do." It was his business. All his plans, visits, studies, sermons, journeys, centred in Christ. Among Jews and Gentiles—in Ephesus and Corinth, at Athens and Rome, among the barbarians of Melita and the sages of the Areopagus, it was all one; he 'knew nothing but Jesus Christ and him crucified.'

History has presented to us various examples of men who have illustrated the power of a single, great, controlling passion. And power of this sort always impresses the mind with a sort of awe, even where it fails to command our moral approbation. Witness, for example, the boundless ambition of Napoleon Buonaparte; or the vast intellectual treasures which made the name of Humboldt a synonym for universal knowledge. Or, take, as a more grateful instance, the favorite representative of philanthropy, John Howard. But no man was ever more completely possessed by a single passion than St. Paul; and the mingled awe and admiration it inspires, is all the greater because the passion which consumed him was the noblest of all passions, the love of Christ. To learn what this sentiment is capable of—what labors it can perform, what sacrifices it can make, what dangers it can dare, what trials it can endure, and what victories it can achieve—it is only needful to study the life of this illustrious apostle. Nor is it possible to do this without the reflection, 'How irresistible would the Church be if all who are marshalled in her ranks could say in the sense in which he said it, To me to live is Christ.'

Such in a measure is the case with every true Christian. In just so far as he is imbued with the genuine spirit of discipleship, it will be 'Christ' for him to 'live.' Instead of making his own honor or advancement the prime end of life, he sets before him the glory of his Master and the welfare of his kingdom. Not only does his conscience impel him to this course, but his affections do also. He adopts it because he finds his happiness in it. The themes with which it makes him conversant, the offices to which it prompts him, and the fruits it yields, are grateful to him. It is a service which he feels to be immeasurably superior to any scheme of life that terminates upon this world. It calls into exercise the best emotions of his nature. It is a perpetual protest against the selfish tendencies which are bound up in every human heart. It gratifies his benevolence. It lifts him above the materialism of earth, and links him in sympathy and aim with the pure spirits of the invisible world. Above all, it keeps his thoughts occupied with the Saviour and his redeeming work, and helps on that growing assimilation to his image, which is the earnest of a future and eternal fellowship with Him in glory.

4. Christ is *the Rule and Standard* of the believer's life.

It need not much surprise us that men in general are no better, when we consider by what rules they live. Water does not rise higher than its fountain; and it were strange if men should soar above their own models. It may not be that every person deliberately proposes to himself a certain standard of excellence, or a specific code of rules for the regulation of his conduct. But there can be no question that the actual standard adopted by people generally is usage or custom. They are content to be as good as their neighbors. If they conform to the prevalent habits of society, they are apt to hold themselves unimpeachable on the score of morals. And when they go beyond this, so far as to superadd to the decorum of life a routine of religious observances, they are slow to believe that they can be seriously at fault either in theory or practice.

The Christian has a different standard. With him, 'to live, is Christ.' The rule he recognizes is, the teachings and the example of Christ. In resolving questions of duty, he is not wont to make his primary appeal to the world. He goes, rather, to the unerring Word and the throne of grace. It may subject him to the charge of singularity; but he would sooner be singular with Christ than sin with the world. When he accepted Jesus as a Saviour, he owned Him no less as a King. He had no thought, and has none now, of sharing in the benefits of his atonement, without acknowledging his authority. In coming to Christ, it was to 'take his *yoke* upon him, and *learn* of Him;' and to refuse to wear his yoke, would be to show that he had not yet come to Him. For this is the Master's own test: "Ye are my friends, if ye do whatsoever I command you."

5. Christ is the *Support and Solace* of the believer's life.

The Christian life is not all duty, nor all privilege. It involves chastisement and affliction with a uniformity which seldom knows an exception. If he requires a plain chart and an inflexible standard to guide his steps, he will as certainly need some unfailing source of consolation. And this is part of that "all in all" which he has in Christ. For who so able or willing to comfort the afflicted? He did not spend thirty years in this vale of tears without learning what sorrow is. That bitter cup He drank to the dregs, as He never requires his people to drink of it. And now when they suffer, their first thought is of their suffering Lord. However they may have neglected Him in health and prosperity, the first stroke of trouble sends them to his feet. The smitten believer cannot stay away from Christ. He turns to Him with an instinct which cannot be repressed. His feeling is—

> "Whither, O whither should I fly,
>   But to my loving Saviour's breast,
> Secure within thine arms to lie,
>   And safe beneath thy wings to rest?"

How many eyes swimming with tears must be turned towards Him at this moment from every land which his Gospel has reached! How many sobbing voices are pouring their griefs into his ear! How many burdened and anxious souls are pleading with Him for deliverance from actual or impending trials! And not one of all these sufferers shall be overlooked by Him. For it is his own comforting assurance, "In the world ye shall have tribulation; but be of good cheer; I have overcome the world."

6. Christ is the *Crown* of the Christian's life.

This belongs to the future. The purport of it is, that He who has been their 'life' all through the changes of this mortal state, will bestow *Himself* upon them hereafter with a glory worthy alike of his exalted rank and of his infinite love to them. He has told us that in the day of days, He will present his Church to Himself as a bride adorned for her husband. These august espousals will take place in the presence of an applauding universe. The Church, refulgent with a glory beyond that of cherubim and seraphim, will be exalted to his right hand with a pomp and joy which have graced no other nuptials; and every blood-bought sinner will feel, that in the consummation of this sublime union with his Lord, his cup of blessing has been filled to overflowing.

Other ideas there are embraced in this comprehensive phrase, "to me to live is Christ;" but let it suffice to have shown that it imports that Christ is the SOURCE of the believer's life; that He is its PRESERVER AND GUARDIAN; its END AND OBJECT; its RULE AND STANDARD; its SUPPORT AND SOLACE; and its immortal CROWN.

This brief exposition of the text may well supersede any formal argument in commending it to you as your watchword for the year. For if the ideas just presented are comprehended in this expression, it must be apparent that it proposes to us the noblest of all ends and the best possible rule of life. It is, therefore, eminently adapted to the purpose contemplated in this discourse,—and that in respect to persons of all classes and conditions. Should the feeling arise in the bosoms of any who hear me, 'It may answer for those who are in more favorable circumstances, and who have ample opportunities for Christian usefulness, to adopt it as their rule, "To me to live is Christ;" but it cannot be material to one in my humble situation to do this,—let me assure you that you have fallen into a serious error. This is no lesson for the rich and the learned merely; no prerogative of the great. Whether considered as a duty or a privilege—and it is really both—it belongs alike to all, and is equally indispensable to all. It is impossible you should be placed in any circumstances where there will not be room for the exercise of this feeling. From the dawn of moral agency until we close our eyes in death, every day and hour brings occasion for us to say, 'To me to live is Christ.'

These beloved children and youth who are at various stages of their education,—there is no reason why you should not carry this sentiment into all your studies and pastimes. I say 'pastimes,' because it is quite needful to have it understood, that religion does not frown upon innocent amusements. It is not Christianity, but the heartless, mercenary spirit of the world, which condemns so many thousands of boys and girls to a joyless childhood. Were the reign of Christianity universally established, there is no portion of the human family who would feel the auspicious change more decidedly than children. Religion is your best friend. If you will enter upon this new year with full purpose of heart to *live for Christ*, you will go about your studies with fresh vigor, your recreations will have a new zest, the circle of your rational pleasures will be enlarged, you will have strength to combat your infirmities of temper, and you will be able to do something for that Saviour who has done everything for you. There are those among you who can verify this representation from their own experience. They will tell you, that there is no life like living for Christ. Would that all the young persons who hear me might consecrate this opening year to God, by resolving in his strength, 'Henceforth it shall be Christ for me to live.'

I speak to many who earn a scanty sustenance by patient toil—at service, perhaps; by the needle; in the workshop or the factory. I shall not greatly err if I assume that you have your share of the crosses and vexations of life. You are brought into contact with untoward tempers, or, peradventure, suffer from them in your own breasts. Or your health wavers. Or the depression of trade abridges your work and wages, while a family look up to you for their daily bread.

'And is this text, then,' you may be ready to ask, 'designed for people like us?' Yes; precisely for such people as you are. Who stand in greater need of just such a monitor? "To me to live is Christ." Take this into your workshop. Take it into the broad thoroughfare where you are pursuing your humble but honest calling. Take it up to your lonely attic where you grow weary and sad over your possibly ill-paid needlework. Open your hearts to the blessed thought, 'My Master has appointed my lot; and He knows what poverty and toil are.' Yes, He does know. He knows all that you suffer, and all that you fear. And He is able to sustain you under every burden; and to reconcile you to the things which most try your patience, and perhaps excite your murmuring. Only admit Him to your daily companionship, and you will be astonished to find that your burdens are more than half gone.

It may mortify and harass you to think that you are spending life for such 'trivial and unworthy ends.' And well it may, if you are living only for the ends which are bound up in your handicraft. Look at that wonderful assemblage of powers and susceptibilities which pertains to man as man, and which divides the very lowest of the race from all the inferior animals; and say whether it is meet that a creature thus endowed with intelligence and conscience and immortality, should spend a score of years, or, as it may be, three score years, at some manual labor with no higher thought or aim than that of keeping himself and his family from starvation. If this be the view you take of your allotment, there must be discontent. But this is the atheistic, not the Scriptural, view. It is no ordinance of the Deity that you should live and die for no better ends than these. Your trade, I grant, may be of his decree. It may be his will that you should turn a lathe, or haul stone, or chop wood, or spool yarn, or make up clothing, and so earn a support for years together. But it is no less his will that you should fulfil these various tasks *because He has prescribed them, and out of love and loyalty to Him.* His requisition is, that we shall do nothing for its own sake merely, or for any earthly end; but everything for Him and to Him. To show how comprehensive this obligation is, He has expressly embraced in it the commonest actions of life—those upon which life itself is suspended. 'Whether, therefore, ye eat or drink, or whatsoever ye do, do all to the glory of God.' This is but another form of the sentiment with which we are dealing. He for whom it is Christ to live, does all to the glory of God. It is the infusion of this element into the world's toil that redeems it from all degradation. As if to silence dispute upon this point, the apostle has applied the principle even to the extreme case of Roman bondmen. The Christian slaves of pagan masters are exhorted to obedience on the ground that the service they pay their owners is really paid to Christ, and that He will reward them for it. "Be obedient . . . as the servants of Christ, doing the will of God from the heart; with good-will doing service as to the Lord, and not to men: knowing that whatsoever good thing any man doeth, the same shall he receive of the Lord, whether he be bond or free." And thus it is that Christianity dignifies and ennobles *all* labor. It matters not how obscure the sphere he has assigned you, nor how completely its material results may be absorbed in the bare support it yields you, if you are traversing your diurnal round with the steadfast aim, 'To me to live is Christ,' there are angels encamped around you, and the Lord of angels will one day say to you, 'Well done, good and faithful servant.'

This same train of remark is equally applicable to those engaged in mercantile life and in the liberal professions. If your pursuits are of a more elevated nature than those just referred to, they are nevertheless open to the same impeachment, as being in themselves utterly unworthy to engross our ultimate aims. There is nothing in commerce, or literature, or the liberal arts, which can fill and satisfy the soul. Not only so, but these occupations may no more exclude the Deity from our plans, than may any other form of idolatry. They have their legitimate place; but they fall into that place only when the heart has been touched with the love of God. It is morally impossible that you should pursue them as they ought to be pursued, until you have learned to say, 'To me to live is Christ.' If you will begin this year with an unreserved consecration of yourselves to Christ, and make it the rule of your conduct to live for Him alone, every day will bring you its reward. I do not say that it will insure you an unexampled measure of outward prosperity, though this would be its proper tendency; but I do say that it would in various ways exert a wholesome influence upon your studies and your business; that it would afford you timely aid in perplexity and temptation; that it would take some of the thorns out of your paths; and that it would make you wiser and better men, and bring you a happier year than many of those which are gone.

In respect to the duties involved in the purpose, "To me to live is Christ," it clearly imports an habitual desire and aim to employ one's talents, time, substance, and opportunities, in promoting the cause and kingdom of Christ in the world.

There are those here who have long made this their

endeavor, and who must in sincerity thank God to-day that they have not entirely failed of their object. But there are probably none present who can recall their past years without a pang of regret. With most of us, indeed, this retrospect must be fruitful of self-upbraidings. For where is the year which has borne to heaven the report it might and should have borne? Who is there that has *made the most of life*, even for a single twelve-month? Let this reflection make us the more solicitous to begin this year aright. Especially let it nerve us to enter upon the year resolved to do all the good we can in the name and for the sake of Christ.

In order to this, the essential thing is to give the Saviour that place in our affections which properly belongs to Him. If He has his place in our hearts, He will have it in our plans, in our conversation, in our labors, and in our lives. One of the most remarkable utterances that ever came from a death-bed, fell from the lips of that saintly philanthropist, Elizabeth Fry, in her last illness. Addressing one of her daughters, she said, "I can say one thing:—Since my heart was touched at seventeen years old, I believe I never have awakened from sleep, in sickness or in health, by day or by night, without my first waking thought being, *how best I might serve my Lord*." And that this was said in no ostentatious spirit, was evident from her constant prayer, that she 'might be humble-minded, and preserved from *decking herself with her Lord's jewels*.'

There is something so wonderful in this, that one is tempted to pause and ponder it. But that we cannot do now. Let it rather show us to what heights of holiness the soul may attain even in our own day, and amidst the stir and bustle of great cities. And let it suggest, as it must to every thoughtful mind, what glorious results would flow from the labors even of a single Church, if all its members could say in the spirit in which Mrs. Fry said it, "To me to live is Christ." The working of such a spirit once lodged in the hearts of a people, would be as certain and decisive as that of leaven put into meal. Should it please God to bestow it upon us, it would evince its presence by tokens which could neither be mistaken nor disparaged. There would be a great waking up—a resurrection as it were—of the slumbering life of the Church. There would be deep contrition and repentance. There would be a revival of brotherly love. There would be a growing attachment to the Sanctuary and the place of prayer. There would be a prompt and cheerful liberality towards the Institutions of the Church. There would be ready workers for the Sunday School, and for the Home Missions of our city. There would be more of household consecration, and the flame would burn more brightly upon many a family altar. There would be frequent conversions; and many would be seen pressing into the kingdom of God. All would feel that they must aid, according to their several gifts, in helping forward the good cause—even those who have hitherto stood aloof, with little more than a nominal connection with the church. And there would be here a scene of unobtrusive, efficient Christian activity, the beneficent results of which it would take an angel's tongue to rehearse, and an eternity to unfold.

Such, my friends, are the fruits it would be reasonable to anticipate, could the purpose be deeply enshrined in all our hearts to-day. "To me to live is Christ." You will judge whether it behooves you to take this as your watch-word, and to try in your Master's name to keep it ever before you.

With one other thought I shall close. I have spoken chiefly of the active portion of the Christian life. Our text includes much more. It meant much more as the Apostle used it. It was as much 'Christ' for him 'to live' in perils and persecutions and prisons, as when he was preaching the Gospel to anxious thousands. In this way, doubtless,—in some school of sorrow or of suffering—it may please God to require some of us to exemplify this precept. Need I remind you that there is no form in which trouble can overtake you during this year, that it will not help to prepare you for the blow and support you under it, to be able to say, "To me to live is Christ?" Let the night be ever so dark and the storm ever so fierce, you cannot be overwhelmed if you are bound by this close and indissoluble tie to the Saviour:— as soon might that boat upon Gennesareth have perished in which He lay asleep amidst his terrified disciples. Whether, therefore, for action or for passion, whether the unknown future is to bring with it health or sickness, joy or sorrow, life or death, I commend it to you as your sacred talisman for this opening year, and I humbly implore God to write it upon our hearts,—

"TO ME TO LIVE IS CHRIST."

1863.

VI.

"WAITING FOR THE COMING OF OUR LORD JESUS CHRIST."

1 CORINTHIANS I. 7.

This text for the year has not been selected without much deliberation. For our circumstances are so peculiar, so sad, so solemn, that I could not but desire to find some brief and comprehensive scripture which might meet the exigencies of the times, and be a help to you through the unknown changes of this opening year.

It is a fundamental doctrine of the Bible, that the Lord Jesus Christ is to 'come again.' Everything around us implies this. The present dispensation is palpably incomplete in itself. The whole course of the world has been marked with such inequalities, wrong has so triumphed over right, and vice over virtue, that we are compelled to regard the present economy as included in one more comprehensive and enduring. This conviction passes into absolute certainty as soon as we open the New Testament. Let it suffice to quote a very few of the numerous passages in which the subject is mentioned. "If I go and prepare a place for you, I will come again and receive you unto myself." "This same Jesus, which is taken up from you into heaven, shall so come in like manner as ye have seen him go into heaven." "The Son of man shall come in the glory of his Father, with his angels; and then shall he reward every man according to his works." "Behold he cometh with clouds, and every eye shall see him." "So Christ was once offered to bear the sins of many; and unto them that look for him shall he appear the second time without sin unto salvation."

His second coming will differ widely from his first. Then He came as an infant. Although angels announced his advent, the world took no notice of his birth. He assumed a very lowly condition. He became a man of sorrows. He was 'despised and rejected of men;' and finally died an ignominious death—fulfilling thus the end for which He stooped to our abode. When He returns, it will be "in the clouds of heaven, with power and great glory." "The Lord himself shall descend from heaven with a shout, with the voice of the archangel, and with the trump of God." Not now a helpless infant; not now a man of sorrows: He comes as a conqueror and Judge. "I saw a great white throne, and him that sat upon it, from whose face the earth and the heaven fled away." "The judgment was set, and the books were opened." "And the dead were judged out of those things that were written in the books, according to their works." And at his irreversible mandate, "the wicked shall go away into everlasting punishment: but the righteous into life eternal."

These passages may serve to shew how the doctrine of the Second advent is interlaced with the whole texture of the New Testament. It was too full of comfort to be kept in the background. The apostles constantly presented it to the churches as a source of encouragement and joy. "Waiting for the coming of our Lord Jesus Christ, who shall also confirm you unto the end, that ye may be blameless in the day of our Lord Jesus Christ." "Yet a little while, and he that shall come, will come, and will not tarry." "Looking for that blessed hope, and the glorious appearing of the great God and our Saviour Jesus Christ." So far from being a speculative sentiment with them, they cherished it as a vital and most precious truth. Their converts did the same. The early Christians lived in the faith of it. Every reader of ecclesiastical history knows what prominence they gave to the doctrine of Christ's second coming, how largely it entered into their religious experience, and how much it helped to mould their characters.

Then, as now, there was much speculation as to the period of this wished-for event. Some of them fell into the error of the Thessalonian Christians, who, misinterpreting a passage in St. Paul's first Epistle to them, supposed that the second advent was just at hand. It was one of the chief objects of the second Epistle to rectify this mistake. But it has been often repeated since. Our own day is rife with confident predictions as to the year, sometimes as to the month and even the day, of the great Epiphany. We have no warrant to censure all inquiries in this direction. The prophecies of Scripture claim our attention, as well as its histories. But this is ground where we must tread softly. Prophecy will not yield its secrets to a proud, inquisitorial temper. When a man begins to dogmatize here, you may safely turn away from him. All that any, the most humble and devout student, can hope for, is to be led into an approximate estimate of the time for our Lord's appearing. Peradventure the time may be very near—as so many voices affirm. Whether near or remote, however, our duty is plain. The Saviour is certainly coming; and it behooves us to await his approach as those who feel that He may be at the door. This is the lesson of the text, and we cannot ponder it too seriously. We are not able to indicate the day when He is to come: the problem baffles our sagacity. But, practically, death and the advent are identical as to our individual experience. To us, Christ's coming is the hour of our departure into his presence. Let us blend the two views, the general and the particular, together, or, as occasion serves, adopt one or the other indifferently, in meditating upon the theme.

It must be apparent from the Scriptures we have quoted that the future advent of Christ is to mark the grand consummation of this world's affairs; and we must therefore recognize his agency in everything that occurs. This observation applies particularly to events of a public nature. These events not unfrequently confound our wisdom. They are not at all in the line which, if that were our prerogative, we should prescribe. They diverge from it, indeed, so widely, that our faith needs to be recruited from above before we can acquiesce in them. No illustration could be more to our purpose here, than the present melancholy condition of our country. It is true, we can trace out the causes which have brought this terrible war upon us. We can distinctly refer it to the passions in which most wars originate. We can indicate the series of measures, the plans, and policies, of leading individuals and of political parties, which preceded and produced it. We can at least partially account in the same way for the disastrous course of the war, which presses like a mill-stone upon all hearts to-day. But this does not meet the case. We need something more to keep down the murmuring and repining which are struggling in so many breasts for utterance. We think of our glorious heritage as it was; and then, through our tears, we look at it as it is. "We are become a reproach to our neighbors, a scorn and derision to them that are round about us." We are made " a by-word among the heathen, a shaking of the head among the people." And there is but one reflection which can relieve the intolerable anguish of our hearts: that is, the thought that God's hand is in all these changes. "These are parts of *his* ways." They belong to that sublime plan He is working out; which comprehends as well cabinets and empires, as the beasts of the field and the fowls of the air. Everything in this plan looks to the coming of the Son of man to judge the world. To this end converge all the agencies concerned in this sad contest, whatever contributed to produce it, and the countless incidents, great and small, which have marked its progress. He foresaw all, permitted all, controls all, and all will be reviewed and adjudicated by Him at his coming.

We may go a step further. I know not how far it may relieve the minds of thoughtful and desponding men, but the Saviour himself has taught us that such scenes as these *must* lead on his advent. When the twelve asked him, 'What shall be the sign of thy coming,' He said, "Ye shall hear of wars and rumors of wars: see that ye be not troubled; for all these things must come to pass, but the end is not yet. For nation shall rise against nation, and kingdom against kingdom, and there shall be famines, and pestilences, and earthquakes, in divers places. All these are the beginning of sorrows." If so, then no strange thing has happened to us. Whatever our pride and self-complacency may have suggested, we had really no reason to expect an exemption from these predicted calamities. And now that they are upon us, our duty is to accept them as part of " the things that must come to pass" before ' the sign of the Son of man' appears ' in heaven.' The true use of them is to impress it more vividly upon our minds that Christ will certainly come again, to engage our thoughts in suitable meditations upon his advent, and to stir up all who know how to pray to intercede with Him on behalf of our afflicted country. If He is leading us as a people ' in a way that we knew not,' if He is ' giving us the bread of adversity and the water of affliction,' let us patiently wait " for the coming of our Lord Jesus Christ," assured that it will clear up the mysteries of this dispensation, and make it subservient to the ultimate triumph of his Church.

The sentences quoted a moment ago have a still broader signification. 'Nation shall rise against nation, and kingdom against kingdom; and there shall be famines, and earthquakes, and pestilences, in divers places.' We are engrossed with our own war. It fixes for the time the attention of the other great powers of Christendom. But if there be any foundation for the belief, so general among Christians, that this prophecy relates to a period not now very distant, it is quite as likely that other nations may be involved in war, as that our fratricidal strife will soon cease. It need not surprise us to see the convulsions which are desolating our country and Mexico, kindling a fire which shall enwrap all Europe, and perhaps the globe, in its baleful splendors. The believer is forewarned. He has 'the sure word of prophecy' to sustain his faith, whatever may happen. With the Psalmist he may say,

> "Let mountains from their seats be hurled
>   Down to the deep, and buried there,
> Convulsions shake the solid world,—
>   Our faith shall never yield to fear.
>
> Loud may the troubled ocean roar :
>   In sacred peace our souls abide,
> While every nation, every shore,
>   Trembles, and dreads the swelling tide."

Of the horrors which may attend these mighty conflicts, and the transformation they are to work in the political geography of the globe, we can form no adequate conception. The only thing certain about them is that He "who hath his way in the whirlwind and in the storm," is at the helm, and will so restrain and guide the turbulent tide of affairs as to make every change subservient to his own infinitely wise purposes. Through all the darkness and terror of the chaos which, it would seem, is to come upon the world, one beam of light will continue to shed its calm, consoling radiance upon the believer's path,—the light that presages and assures the second coming of his Lord. Here he finds comfort when all around him are in despair. It is not that he is insensible to the claims of his country and his race. Humanity and patriotism draw their noblest inspirations from the bosom of Christianity. But however sacred may be these ties, he has others that are higher and holier still. He belongs to 'a kingdom that cannot be moved;' a kingdom which he knows will survive these commotions, and to the strength and splendor of which they will even be made to contribute. It is his daily prayer that this 'kingdom' may 'come.' And nothing will help so much to reconcile him to the 'wars and rumors of wars,' the 'earthquakes and pestilences' which are to afflict the nations, as the conviction that they herald the "coming of the Lord Jesus Christ."

Thus much it seemed proper to say respecting the bearing of this text upon public affairs. The times that are passing over us are fraught with such momentous issues, are so full of solemn warning and instruction, that no Year-text could be appropriate which might not aid us in interpreting and submitting to them. I know of nothing better that we can do in reference to these sad and appalling scenes than to fix our thoughts upon the great event of the future, and, with lowly reverence and steadfast trust, wait "for the coming of the Lord Jesus Christ."

But this text has other lessons for us of a more personal character. First of all, it suggests the importance of *preparing to meet the Lord* at his coming. This is implied in 'waiting' for Him. The parable of the ten virgins shows that we may go out to meet Him, without being ready for Him. The five foolish virgins who went forth with the wise, represent, it is to be feared, multitudes who bear the lamp of a Christian profession with no oil in it— no grace. Nor will the most serious and faithful believers ever feel themselves to be so well prepared for his coming, that they might not be more so. Nothing, in this view, could be more helpful, than the habitual looking for his advent to which the text refers; as nothing, certainly, could be more rational. For, as already hinted, the advent which directly concerns us as individuals is that in which He comes to summon us into eternity. He has himself connected with it the admonition I am enforcing: "*Be ye also ready ;* for in such an hour as ye think not *the Son of man cometh.*" What could more effectually put us upon instant and constant exertions to prepare for this event, than the conviction that it may occur at any moment? Impressed with this feeling—daily awaiting the Son of man—there is no one who would not examine carefully his foundations, to learn whether his hope would be likely to bear the scrutiny of the Omniscient eye. It would quicken our solicitude in this direction, to reflect that many are self-deceived; that there are tares among the wheat; that many will seek at the last day to enter in who shall not be able; and that many who will in that day stand and cry 'Lord, Lord,' will hear from his lips the overwhelming reply, 'I never knew you.' These and other considerations show the necessity of an honest and prayerful inquest into the grounds of our hope. When He comes, He will try that hope. He will see whether it rests only upon his own blood and righteousness; whether it has 'purified the heart' as He is pure; and whether it is attended by faith and humility and the other Christian graces. And every one who desires to guard against a mistake, will anticipate this scrutiny, and bring his hope to the unerring test of Holy Scripture.

Nor this alone. No one who is waiting and longing for his Master's appearing, will be satisfied to rest here. The deeper his conviction that he is " in Christ," the more resolutely will he strive to be like Christ. The expectation of meeting an earthly monarch, surrounded with the splendors of a court, may exhaust itself in laborious preparations to *appear* well. The King of kings cannot be put off with a show of outward grace and dignity. To meet Him acceptably, we must not simply appear, but be, what He can approve. It is the property and the high privilege of his people to bear something of his image. And those who wait for his coming will deem no pains too great, and no sacrifices too severe, which may bring them into closer fellowship with their Lord, and impart to them more of his likeness. If you give this text its proper place in your hearts for the coming twelve-month, or so much of the period as it may please God to spare you, you will be growing like Him daily, and his advent will fill you with ' joy unspeakable.'

Not less potential will it prove *as a stimulus to duty.* The argument here is very short. 'The Son of man is coming back. He may appear at any hour. Let me, then, do with my might whatever my hands find to do.' This argument is conclusive in whatever aspect we contemplate Him. We may await Him as our final Judge. Then it behooves us to abound in those offices of kindness and sympathy which He himself has taught us will receive his benediction at the last day:—" Inasmuch as ye have done it unto one of the least of these my brethren, ye have done it unto me." We may await Him as our Sovereign. This world, then, is a part of his domain. He has placed us here that we may help to bring it back to its allegiance. To one He has given five talents; to another two; to another one. To each He has said, ' Go work in my vineyard.' We may look to his return as our Saviour. Then we owe Him our all. What boundless love was that which brought Him down to Bethlehem, which led Him to Gethsemane and Calvary for our redemption! Let this ineffable love 'constrain' us. Let us live for Him who died for us!

This is the natural, necessary effect of waiting for his advent. Our work is large. He it is that prescribed it, who alternately commands and entreats us not to neglect it. The obligation to prosecute it with unfaltering step, borrows increased sanctity from the manger and the cross; from his first advent to ransom his people, and his future advent to crown them with glory and honor and immortality. It is a work every way worthy of the nature and destiny of the race. It is as vast and enduring as the soul. It looks to the well-being of man here and hereafter. It links itself with the clemency and the benevolence of the Deity. And yet it admits of the co-operation—it demands the co-operation—of all, down to the very humblest; of those who have but a single talent, or who can cast but their two mites into his treasury. This work, I say, He has laid upon us all. It lies around us in every direction. It is in our houses. It fringes the paths we are every day traversing. It appeals to our strongest sympathies, for it is the case of the diseased, of the wounded, of the dead. If they were the victims of the battle field, the poor, spectral inmates of the hospital, we could not refuse them our aid. In part, they are. For this is just one department of the service to which He is now calling us. But it is not the whole. "The field is *the world.*" Where there is bodily sickness, and where there is not; wherever there is *sin*, there the 'field' is; there lies our work—broad enough, varied enough, difficult enough, momentous enough, to task the powers of angels, yet to be done by us or not done at all.

Very many, and very cogent are the arguments which commend this service to us. But the one reflection we are more concerned with is, that "the Lord Jesus *shall so come*, in like manner" as the twelve saw Him "go into heaven." To believe this, to realize it, to take it with us into all the hours and all the scenes of this opening year, would supersede all the appeals and expostulations with which we are accustomed to chide our own and each other's delays, and mould our Christianity to a type which, peradventure, it has never yet put on. What further need of exhortation, with a people whose faith habitually sees their Lord, however distant, coming in the clouds of heaven to judge the world? What element of greater power could be infused into the heart of any believer?

This earnest, constant longing for the advent would make 'new creatures' of us all. It would reduce the things of earth, its cares, its plans, its honors, to something of their true dimensions. It would dissolve the spell which makes so many of us live as if the things which are not seen were temporal, and the things which are seen, eternal. It would reprove our ready discouragement on meeting with difficulties, and our timidity in the presence of dangers. It would set every one of us to work in some way; not to do each other's tasks, but our own; not spending life in useless regrets that we have not the gifts and opportunities of some one else, but employing the gifts and opportunities the Master has bestowed upon us to the best possible advantage. What energy it would infuse into every bosom! What a new aspect it would spread over the face of this, or any other church—this conscious, pervading sense of the coming of the Lord Jesus Christ! How it would clothe the preaching and the hearing with new solemnity! How it would crowd the prayer-meeting with devout worshippers! How it would lift all Sabbath-school teaching up into a region of spiritual vitality! How it would swell indefinitely the willing offerings to the Lord's treasury! How it would arouse formal and useless professors to the realities of the Christian life! How it would enkindle the sympathies of God's people and call forth their exertions on behalf of the unconverted! How it would send forth new workers into every department of missionary and philanthropic labor, among the poor, the sick, the vicious, and the lost! How it would exorcise the envy and the jealousy and the pride which now infest even the Church itself, and cement into one the blessed brotherhood of the faithful! How, by God's blessing, it would bring down showers of heavenly influence upon the Church, and lead on those promised Pentecostal seasons when converts shall fly to Zion 'as clouds, and as doves to their windows!' Is it not worth while, with interests like these at stake, to give 'the coming of our Lord Jesus Christ' its due place in our hearts and lives?

This text, again, will meet an urgent want: it will be to you a *well-spring of consolation*. 'An urgent want,' I call this, for such, alas, it is. Every year must needs bring its sorrows: for 'man is born to trouble as the sparks fly upward.' But these are years of '*great tribulation.*' Look at the symbols of woe here, and in every church you enter, and along all the thoroughfares. If we could bring the mourners of the land together they would make an army larger than that which has gone forth for the protection of our Constitution, and every battle is swelling their crowded ranks—adding fresh widows and orphans to the mighty concourse of the bereaved. Nor is this work likely to cease. Whatever may be the case with the forces in the field, this army of mourners bids fair to go on recruiting its sombre columns with unslacked energy. You need, then—we *all* need, for who is not a sharer in these sorrows? we need for this year which literally opened with blood and carnage,* some word of grace and hope from the sacred oracles which may strengthen us for these trials. We have it here: "Waiting for the coming of our Lord Jesus Christ." For this assures us that these scenes must have an end. We are almost despairing of this. Every one is asking of his neighbor, 'Is this war ever to end?' The manner in which it has been conducted gives but too much occasion for this feeling. But it will end—in God's own time and way. Sooner or later it must give place to a widely-different dispensation,—for the introduction of which, as already intimated, it is a necessary part of the preparation. And whatever may be the Divine purpose respecting the future course of the war, you can have no better antidote for its griefs than to fix your minds trustfully upon the coming of Christ. To us individually, let me repeat, his coming is the hour of our departure out of this world. If we can but get our hearts filled with this thought, with the sense of his approach, with the patient looking and longing for Him, we might survey even these harrowing scenes with something of serenity. The

---

* The battle of Murfreesboro', Tenn.

secret of that composure which so many martyrs have displayed at the stake and in the arena of wild beasts, lay in their confident persuasion of Christ's coming. Nor is this a gift confined to times of persecution. It is lighting up many a death-bed around us with rays from his 'far-off coming.' It is the common heritage of his people, if they only have the faith to appropriate it. What power can earth or hell have to harm a believer who sees and desires the coming of his Saviour? This event is so sublime in its nature, so vast in its proportions, that where it is fitly realized and appreciated, it must absorb all other events. To see and feel it as the apostle whose language we are using did, is to be armed against all adversaries. It was this faith which enabled him to say, "I take pleasure in infirmities, in reproaches, in necessities, in persecutions, in distresses, for Christ's sake." "I am filled with comfort; I am exceeding joyful in all our tribulations." He could say these things because he 'waited for the Son of God from heaven'— patiently and confidently 'looking for that blessed hope, and the glorious appearing of the great God and our Saviour Jesus Christ.' Could we emulate his faith in this doctrine, we should attain his composure and joy in danger and suffering. There is no reason why we should not attempt this. The circumstances we are placed in make it peculiarly our duty, yes, and our privilege, too, to dwell more upon this great event, which St. Paul and the early Christians found such a source of comfort. The turmoil and strife around us bid us lift our thoughts from the temporal to the spiritual, from man to God, from earth to heaven. It is an inexpressible relief to turn away from all this sin and suffering and sorrow, from the confusion and wreck and chaos of earth, to that pure and animating and glorious contemplation,— the Saviour of the world coming to take his ransomed people home. If this brings no balm to your wounded hearts, I know not what will solace you.

For Christ's coming, as just hinted, is for a purpose. To await his advent, is to have the thoughts engaged with what is to follow it—that is, *with heaven*. And if ever there was a time with us, when those who 'love his appearing' might well employ themselves in meditating upon heaven, that time is the present. We cannot afford to dispense with it. To shut us up to earth; to compel us to fix our thoughts day by day and hour by hour, without relief, upon the calamities which are blighting and blasting our beloved country, were to consign us all to hopeless despondency and wretchedness. Heaven tenders us the respite that we need. The deeper the shadows which gather around us, the more grateful its chastened light. The louder swells the voice of battle and the wail of mourners, the more welcome its cloudless peace and seraphic anthems. The sharper our griefs and the sadder the blighting of our earthly hopes, the more fondly should we turn to that bright abode where God shall wipe away all tears from all eyes, and 'sorrow and sighing shall flee away.'

Surely, nothing can be more consoling to Christian mourners, nothing more becoming to all Christians at a season like the present, than devout meditation upon the Saviour's coming, and the glory which is to follow it. What we require, what we should fervently pray for, is, that the Divine Spirit may not only write this blessed text upon our memories, but imbue our whole nature with it;

that He may keep it ever before our minds, that the Saviour will come again; that He may help us to live in the faith of this precious truth ; and that amidst all the untried experiences of this year, its duties and its perils, its anxieties and its temptations, its pleasures and its sorrows, He may enable us patiently and hopefully to "wait for the coming of our Lord Jesus Christ," and daily to grow in meekness for a holy and happy heaven.

If I have chiefly spoken, in these remarks, to and of the communion of the faithful, it has been with no design of excluding the rest of my people from the scope of this exhortation. To you, my unconverted friends, no less than to professing Christians, I tender it as your motto for the year, "waiting for the coming of our Lord Jesus Christ." To you, I might almost say, by pre-eminence I commend it. That you have never yet walked in the light of such a text, is a most cogent reason why you should adopt it now. That his coming concerns you as much as it concerns his own people; that it concerns you more deeply than any other future event; that your concern in it will continue as the absorbing interest of your being while eternity rolls on its endless cycles; are truths to which you will readily assent. If truths at all, they are truths of infinite moment to you. Why not, then, enter upon this new year by fixing your thoughts upon the Second advent? Why not take this as your guiding star for the year? The fact of Christ's coming is indisputable. Should not a fact which is to draw such vast issues after it be recognized in your plans, in your business, in your domestic and social relations, in the whole routine of life? Can you hope for mercy through the blood of Christ, if you refuse to acknowledge Him? Is it not better to wait for Him as a Saviour, than to meet Him as a Judge? to surrender to his love, than to be overwhelmed by his vengeance? God grant that you may so ponder these things, as to spend this year, " WAITING FOR THE COMING OF OUR LORD JESUS CHRIST."

1864.

VII.

"APPROVED UNTO GOD."

2 TIMOTHY ii. 15.

This you will please accept as our year-text. If we make it such in reality, it cannot fail to impress upon this new year, or upon so much of it as we may be spared to see, a value which, perhaps, few of our years have borne.

It is the parting counsel of 'Paul the aged' to his 'son Timothy,—his 'parting counsel,' for this his latest Epistle was written just before his martyrdom. "Study to show thyself approved unto God, a workman that needeth not to be ashamed, rightly dividing the word of truth." He knew that this young Evangelist, to whom he was bound by so many tender ties, would be called to a life of great labor and trial; and that no efforts would be wanting on the part of the subtle adversaries of the Gospel, to drive or entice him into forbidden paths. As a safeguard against these perils, he prescribes for him a rule of duty, so simple, so just, so comprehensive, that no occasion could arise on which he might not find his advantage and comfort in appealing to it. "Study to show thyself approved unto God."

If this was a good rule for Timothy, it must be equally good for us. What I have to propose is, that we carry this sentiment with us into all the scenes and all the engagements of the year; that we begin every morning with the inquiry, 'How can I approve myself unto God to-day?' and ask ourselves every evening, 'How have I approved myself unto God to-day?' that so, the *thought of God* may pervade and hallow the whole course and current of our lives.

This is what I suppose to be fairly included in the exhortation before us. A lofty requisition it certainly is. Flesh and blood cannot compass it. It runs athwart all our native passions; and if our own strength were our only reliance, we might as well attempt to create a sphere as to comply with it. But this is not our dependence. He who calls us to the service, offers us free access to his resources: and these are higher than heaven, and deeper than hell. When He says, 'Ask, and ye shall receive:' 'My grace is sufficient for thee:' 'I will never leave thee nor forsake thee:'—He pledges to his people all the aid they can possibly need in striving to approve themselves unto God. It is in the faith of promises like these that we are to address ourselves to this work. Undertaken and prosecuted in this spirit, the feeblest among us need not shrink from the greatness of the task; while the strongest is not strong enough to attempt it in his own might.

Among the considerations by which this rule may be commended to our adoption, it will be sufficient to mention a very few.

1. It is no arbitrary rule, but one which springs necessarily from the relation in which we stand to God. The primary obligation of all creatures to the Creator, is one of those intuitive truths which no reasoning can make

more palpable. Not to demand their supreme homage, would be for the Deity to abdicate his throne. The perfection of his being requires that every intelligence He forms, should make his will the guide and his glory the end of every action. "For of Him, and through Him, and to Him, are all things."

2. It is the only rule worthy of our powers. Even if it involved no sin, it were an indignity to our rational nature to live for any inferior object. If God did not forbid, there is a witness in our own bosoms that would protest against it. It may be, and probably is, a very subordinate place in the scale of intelligent beings, which is allotted to man. But his present position is no index to his actual endowments. Growth is the law of our existence. An infant of a few days has less intelligence than its contemporary of almost any of the brute races. But the germ of intellect enshrined in that tiny, helpless form, indestructible by the law of its creation, is, by the same law, made susceptible of an indefinite expansion. See in a Milton or an Edwards what a stature it may reach even here, clogged with a perishable body, and exposed to sin and suffering. Can we doubt that this development is to go on with an accelerated energy when the soul ascends to the great Source of truth and becomes the companion of angels? He who should presume to fix a limit to the possible acquisitions of an intelligence like the human soul, would shew himself a traitor to his own nature. We must estimate man more by what he may become in the vast cycles of eternity. And viewing him in this light, it were in derogation of the essential dignity of his nature to make the honour and will of any creature the end and rule of his being. In God alone

can he find a position equal to his capacities; and only by striving to approve himself unto God, can his faculties be properly unfolded and matured for the high destiny that awaits him.

3. It is a further commendation of this rule that, as distinguished from all others, it is simple, uniform, and stable. Occasions may arise, on which one who desires to approve himself unto God may be involved in some perplexity. But a conscientious inquirer will not ordinarily be left long in the dark. The will of God—the rule prescribed in the text—is to be gathered from his word, his providence, and his Spirit. Chiefly are we to seek it in his word. And whatever difficulties may attach to the interpretation of certain parts of Scripture, the Bible is, on the whole, a plain book. Its vital doctrines have disclosed themselves to myriads of children and unlettered peasants; and its moral precepts are written as with a sunbeam. If in respect to any point whether of faith or practice, an inquirer is embarrassed, he has but to ask, and the aid of an infallible Teacher is promised him. The code thus furnished him is uniform and permanent. It utters the same voice in all lands and to all people. It speaks to-day, as it spake eighteen centuries ago. It is independent of human authority. It concedes nothing to erudite skepticism or popular clamor; nothing to the throne or to the altar. Knowing neither fear nor favor, subject to no perturbation, and deferring to no other power, it stands from age to age unchanged amidst a changing world,—a rock forever swept by the waves of human passion, and forever unmoved.

As in contrast with this rule of life, very many adopt as their guide some earthly end or standard. Multiform as these are, they may be reduced to a unit, for they are stems from the same root. *The will of God: the will of man:*—this comprehends the whole. With or without conscious purpose, we all choose God's will or man's, as the law of our lives. For the latter properly comprehends supreme devotion to the world in whatever form. Where we are not serving the Creator, we are serving the creature. If we do not worship the true God, we worship some idol. "Approved unto God," or approved unto man:—this divides the race. And how untowardly for the latter class, must be apparent at a glance. For considered as a rule of duty, the will of man has not one attribute to recommend it. It is without authority: for the Lawgiver has never delegated this control over man's conscience, to his fellows. As the will of a depraved and benighted race, it lacks the first element of an ethical code, rectitude. To follow it would be oftener to do wrong than right. It is fluctuating and uncertain. It varies perpetually—is one thing in this country, and another in that; one thing to-day, and another to-morrow. Who can trim his sails to the capricious gales of popular favor? Or who can surrender himself to the sway of his selfish passions—making his own will the rule of his life—without discovering very soon that he is serving a most arbitrary master? It is a service, too, as hurtful to the character and as fatal to true happiness, as the opposite service is elevating and satisfying.

4. This, indeed, should be mentioned as a distinct and cardinal merit of the rule enjoined in the text—its beneficent influence upon the character. We shall see this as we go on; as we shall, no less, the injurious effects of the opposite rule. But it may be observed here, that no

one can faithfully adopt as his motto, the sentiment, "approved unto God," without reaping from it the most substantial benefits. For, not to speak of the affluent blessings direct from the Divine hand to which such an one becomes heir, the principle thus enthroned in the heart has a ready affinity for whatsoever things are pure, lovely, and of good report. It is essentially restraining, invigorating, elevating, and comforting. It is usually marked by a waking up of dormant and neglected powers. And this is what we all need. For who is there that has not more than one talent laid by in a napkin? Here and there an honorable exception may be noted; but, for the most part, it is only a partial and precarious service we render to God. Instead of 'bringing *all* the tithes into his storehouse,' we too often pacify conscience by offering Him the 'blind and the lame and the sick for sacrifice.' The time is yet to come when the Church shall lay all her treasures at the Saviour's feet. But this day is dawning upon him who strives in good faith to live "approved unto God." For he will rouse himself from his slumber, and take all his gifts of heart and mind,—his intellectual powers and his affections, his learning and experience, his taste and culture, his time and opportunities,—and present them to his Master, with the humble prayer, 'What will thou have me to do?'

Such a disciple will not neglect the due cultivation of his powers. Whatever they may be, they are entrusted to him that he may improve and use them. The possession of a gift carries this obligation with it, as it often decides one's profession for life. One man is plainly designated of God to be a painter, another a sculptor, a third a physician, a fourth an astronomer, and so on.

These are special cases which interpret themselves. But in *all* cases the law in the text requires that we cultivate our several endowments to the very best of our ability, and that we do our work in the best style we can command. This will be the feeling and aim of those who have sincerely accepted it as their maxim, "approved unto God." And living under the habitual pressure of a force at once so powerful and so ameliorating, they will increase rapidly in knowledge and holiness, and the 'joy of the Lord' will be their 'strength.'

5. It may be added once more, in commendation of this rule, that it proposes the only scheme of life which can fit us for the duties and trials of the present world, or prepare us for the happiness of heaven.

But I waive this topic. It will recur incidentally, as will the other topics that have been touched upon in connection with the application of the rule before us to our several relations and interests. We have learned what the rule imports; and, adopting it as our motto for this opening year, we are now to inquire what it may require of us in respect to some few of the experiences which the year will be likely to bring with it.

We begin with the most important of all, *our religious belief*, but only to say a word or two.

The world is full of sects and creeds; not, as to many of them, differing radically from one another, but all contributing to make up that scene of confusion which is so embarrassing to a seeker after truth. There would be slight encouragement to set out on such a quest if it were necessary to go the round of all the churches and investigate the history and the tenets of each of them. Happily, this perplexing service is not laid upon us. Faith is a personal act, an exercise of the individual, not of the multitude. The concurrence of a large, intelligent, and devout denomination in a particular creed or confession may properly commend it to our favorable consideration, but we need some other warrant for our faith. It must not stand in the wisdom of men, but in the power of God. The simple canon by which we are to be guided in this inquiry is, "approved unto God." What has God taught? Is this doctrine contained in his word? Does it come to me inscribed with, 'Thus saith the Lord?' Here is the test of truth. All else is as the small dust of the balance. It is the Divine injunction, 'Prove all things: hold fast that which is good.' And pursuing your researches in this spirit, resolved, as He may assist you, simply to approve yourselves to God in the matter of your belief, and diligently studying the Scriptures, you *will* be guided into the truth.

In framing our schemes of life there is large room for the exercise of this rule. The toiling masses, it is true, have no room for choice. Their scheme of life is made for them, and they have to accept it, as the patient ox bows his neck to the yoke. But are they, therefore, released from the obligation of this rule, or excluded from its advantages? Far from it. It is at once the imperative duty and the high privilege of all the tribes of labor to make it the controlling principle of their lives, "approved unto God." They are no less the subjects of his government; no less the objects of his care than those who are clothed in purple and fine linen. Nor is it less in their power to glorify his name. For all true service is really paid "to the Lord, and not to men." And this is the spirit which should be carried into every sphere of manual labor,—into all the mines and workshops and manufactories of the world, and wherever there are toiling men or toiling women and children. "Approved unto God!" Could you hang this up over all your lathes, and looms, and forges, and engines; let me rather say, could you have it securely lodged in your hearts by Him who alone can put anything good within us, what a new world it would open to you! How much it would do to absolve your labor from the primeval curse, and smooth your rugged paths, and diffuse a sweet serenity through your breasts, and reconcile you to the allotments of Providence, and endear to you the precious words and the patient suffering of Him who 'had not where to lay his head!" If you have not yet made proof of it, if you have been working year after year with no master but iron necessity, and no reward but your scant wages, suppose you come up out of this subterranean prison-life into the nobler sphere of Christian service, where you can see the light of your Father's face, and hear his loving voice, and feel that you have something to live for. He will help you out of your bondage if you ask Him. And then if you will cast away your own wisdom, and the maxims which have hitherto controlled you, and make it throughout this year the one settled principle of your lives, "approved unto God," your repining will all be turned to thankfulness, and your mourning to praise.

To advert to other classes:—you have your plans of life, comprehending your several avocations, the distribution of your time, and other particulars. These plans may or may not have been deliberately framed; enough that they are practically adopted. May the question be allowed, 'Have you submitted them to God's approval?

Have you consulted Him as to all your habits and methods? And do you see the hours speed away with the feeling that they have been spent as He would have had you spend them?' If so, nothing remains to be suggested on this point. But if otherwise, suppose you pause long enough to revise your schemes of life by the light of this simple maxim, "approved unto God." It may be that, holding this lamp in your hands, you will detect some mistakes which you will be glad to rectify. You may discover hours habitually surrendered to sleep or sloth, which ought to be reclaimed. You may learn that you are allowing a wretched parsimony to prescribe the time that shall be devoted to your private religious duties; and that, unless your household altars be repaired, they will soon fall to pieces. You may find that the irresistible tide of business is steadily extending its encroachments into the realm of your domestic life, and threatening to submerge your every social, and almost your every spiritual, interest. You may find that the things that are seen have usurped the place which belongs to the things that are not seen; that the current of worldliness has been imperceptibly swaying you away from your only safe anchorage; and that, however it may fare with your estate, your spiritual husbandry has more the meagre aspect of a field left for the gleaners, than one that has not yet felt the sickle. I do not affirm that this would be the result. But it might prove so with some of us. And, in any event, it must be of wholesome tendency to look into our plans for the opening year and see whether we are able with a good conscience to impress upon every one of them the pregnant inscription, "approved unto God."

In commenting upon the usurpations of business, I mean no disparagement of its just claims. But the reference may fitly remind us that here is another sphere into which it is all-important to carry the sentiment, "approved unto God." Of the duties and dangers, the privileges and responsibilities, of a commercial life, I have spoken to you so fully in a series of lectures which is within your reach, that you will not expect me at any time to go into the subject again in detail. But I *must* press this inspired rule upon the business men here. And, if your kindness will indulge me, I will do it by quoting a brief paragraph from the volume just mentioned, which falls in precisely with the aim of this discourse.

'There may be those who will deem it a very superfluous and a very puritanical procedure to undertake to set up the Bible as the grand regulator of commerce. But how is commerce to be exempted from its jurisdiction? Who is empowered to say, 'We will have the Bible in our houses, our schools, our churches, our charities; but it shall not come into our stores. We are quite willing to live by it, and to die by it, and to go to heaven by it; but, as to trafficking by it, that is out of the question.' It may well happen that to subject the entire business world to this regimen, to replace prescription, usage, expediency, and every spurious rule, with the precepts of Scripture, would lead to inconvenience and losses. It might require some persons to abandon the business they are engaged in, and abridge the profits of others. But what alternative is there? "I had rather be right," said one of our great statesmen a few years ago,—and the remark is quoted oftener than anything he ever said,— "I had rather be right than be President." You all applaud the sentiment. You honor the memory of Henry Clay because he uttered it. We do but apply it to your own profession when we insist upon your enthroning it in your counting-houses. We press it upon you as the one controlling, unalterable, indispensable rule of life, that you *do right*. It may demand sacrifices. It may cost you many a trial of feeling. It may separate you from friends. It may expose you to reproach. These are serious evils. They are to be shunned, if they can be, with a good conscience. But, if you have to choose between them and a good conscience, you cannot be at a loss where truth and duty lie. It is not necessary that you should escape trouble, but it is necessary that you should do right;* in other words, let me add, it is necessary that, in all the plans and transactions of your counting-rooms and factories, you should study to show yourselves "approved unto God." And if you do this, whatever may be its financial results, you will hereafter review this year with grateful praise to the Giver of all good.

Nor is this lesson designed only for the walks of commerce. It pertains to all professions and employments, to both sexes, and to all ages. The purport of it is that we are to pursue our respective avocations in the way which we believe God will sanction. The precept was given to Timothy for the regulation of his studies and preaching: "Study to show thyself approved unto God, a workman that needeth not to be ashamed, rightly dividing the word of truth." In other words, so preach as to secure God's approval. And of course, if it belong

---

* "The Bible in the Counting-house," Lecture II.

to ministers to preach thus, it must belong equally to the people to hear thus. The obligation is reciprocal; we are to preach and to hear just as well as we know how, for our common Master will be satisfied with nothing less. The same is true of the other professions. It is no more the duty of a minister of the Gospel than of a lawyer, a physician, a teacher, to adhere to it as the rule of their lives, "approved unto God." They are asking themselves, 'What do I owe to my pupil, my patient, my client?' But they may satisfy these parties and yet fail in their duty. The paramount question is, 'What does God require of me?' for all duty terminates in God. And while this question must be variously answered, according to the circumstances of each particular case, it may facilitate the solution to have it impressed upon the mind, that He will have us carry into any sphere to which He may appoint us our best abilities, and do our work thoroughly, looking to Him for help, and feeling that his favor is the noblest of all rewards.

But another department claims our notice. We must carry our rule into the domain of *politics*. I do not mean by this simply that statesmen and professed politicians are of right bound by this rule, but that we ought all to recognize it in our several relations and functions as citizens. We can none of us escape from our obligations to the State. It were ungenerous to desire to do so. The Church alone excepted, there is no institution fraught with such manifold blessings to mankind as a wise and just government faithfully administered. We have had experience of this beyond almost any other people. Common gratitude, therefore, demands that we do all in our power to preserve our constitution and liberties inviolate, and to promote generally the well-being of our country. Had the Christian men of the country been true to this trust in past years, this fatal war would have been averted. It may be one of the dearly-bought lessons of the war to teach such men the sacred duty of carrying it into the whole routine of civil life as their guiding principle, "approved unto God."

This obligation comprehends the formation and expression of our political opinion, the exercise of the right of suffrage, the maintenance of the just authority of the magistracy, submission to the laws, the repression of treason and rebellion, and the furthering of such measures as we believe to be adapted to preserve intact our civil charters, and to secure the inestimable privileges we have enjoyed to those who are to come after us. In reference to these and their kindred duties, we have no right to defer to any other rule than this,—"approved unto God." However common it may be to divorce politics and religion, we cannot sanction the disjunction without so far contemning the supremacy of the great Lawgiver; for He has no more exempted the State from his jurisdiction than the Church.

Let it be understood, then, that we are responsible to God for our political sentiments and conduct, and that these are to be regulated by a reverential regard to his word and will. Here is our standard, as distinguished from all spurious standards. The only one of these to which I shall advert is *party*. I am not going to declaim against the existence of political parties. They are the legitimate and salutary fruit of free institutions. The absence of parties is the badge of a despotism; for the manacled are always passive. It must also be conceded that conscientious men will ordinarily be able to act in the main with some party,—the only way in which they can aid effectively in sustaining, modifying, or reversing the current policy. But implicit devotion to a party in all its plans and expedients, concurrence in its theories and measures, purely because they come from the party mint, and have the party brand,—this is not only unworthy of any freeman, but it is incompatible with loyalty to God. He who thus sells himself to a party must make up his mind not only to some very irksome things, but to things of a very equivocal morality. He will have to support men and measures that are offensive to him; and he may even be required to repudiate principles he has held all his life, and adopt others which he has always reprobated.

It must in candor be admitted that the opposite course also has its inconveniences. Men who think for themselves on political subjects, and who carry their religion into their politics, framing their opinions on public affairs with a predominant regard to the Divine will, and resolved never to sacrifice reason and conscience to popularity, must count upon being traduced where they ought to be commended. Refusing to bow to the mandates of party, or to succumb to the passions of the hour, they are usually misapprehended and taunted by men of all parties. Nor need it occasion them any surprise if they even incur the reproaches of friends. If you mean to be conscientious and independent in your politics, you will have to school your sensibility to censure, whether from friends or foes. A painful thing it certainly is to have your fidelity to God requited with the estrangement of those who may have had a warm place in your affections.

But, if the alternative is forced upon you, you have no right to hesitate. This was familiar ground to St. Paul, and here was his mode of meeting it:—" With me it is a very small thing that I should be judged of you or of man's judgment." " For do I now persuade men or God? or do I seek to please men? for if I yet pleased men, I should not be the servant of Christ."

The afflicted condition of our country invests this topic with so much interest, and you will have to act upon it so constantly throughout the year, that I may be allowed to illustrate the principle of the text, in its application to public affairs, by an example drawn from modern history. The name and fame of William Wilberforce belong to the Christian world. On his first entrance into the House of Commons, which he astonished and captivated by his singular eloquence, Mr. Pitt took him cordially by the hand, and gave him his friendship and his confidence. A generous intimacy sprang up between them. After the lapse of five years, during which Wilberforce had given his unvarying and powerful support to the measures of his friend, he found himself compelled to dissent from his policy on the French war. He foresaw the consequences, and would gladly have averted them. He knew that his steadfast adherence to the administration on all other points would go for nothing if he drew back on the particular question then pending; that his motives would be impugned; that the opposition would exult over what would be represented as his defection from the government; and that he must even count upon the personal alienation of his cherished friend, the great minister. But none of these things moved him. He had decided upon his course with the most careful deliberation—even observing a day of fasting and prayer, that he might suitably invoke wisdom and strength from above. And then he went forward sadly, but resolutely, to the work his conscience had laid upon him. He made his speech, and was in no way surprised at the result. The trials he had anticipated, came; and "they were increased by the expressed disagreement of almost all those personal friends with whom he most freely communicated upon political questions, and by the concurrent accounts they forwarded him, from different parts of the country, of the disapprobation of his conduct generally felt by sober-minded men." Most bitter of all the ingredients in this cup, was the estrangement of Pitt; who, to his honor be it spoken, felt the trial beyond almost any other of his life. For it is recorded of him that in his whole public career there were but two events which were able to disturb his sleep,—the mutiny at the Nore, and "the first open opposition of Mr. Wilberforce." It will interest you to know, that this inflexible fidelity to Christian principle received its reward even here. For only a brief six months had passed, before the illustrious statesman became an avowed convert to Wilberforce's views, and their old friendship was renewed.

I place this example before you the more readily, because there has never been a period in our own history when this high moral principle was more needed in our politics than it is now. The influence you can exert in helping to bring this war to an end may be great or small: that is not material. But it is material that it spring from a patriotism which draws its inspiration not from earth but from heaven; not from the public Journals, not from Legislative debates, not from the magistracy, not from your friends, but from God. Only aim, like Wilberforce, to show yourselves, in all your political sentiments and conduct, 'approved unto God;' and however it may fall with you for the time, that country to which we all owe so much, and for whose unity, peace, and lasting prosperity, we should be willing to make any sacrifice compatible with our duty to God, will one day appreciate and honour your fidelity to her cause.

It is no violent transition if we venture for a moment or two into the realm of *social life*. A broad realm it is, comprehending all questions of dress, furniture, entertainments, friendships, amusements, and many other matters. A great and rare achievement it would be to bring this wide field of restless, ever-changeful activity, into complete accord with that high prescription, "approved unto God." How much the adoption of this rule would simplify the mechanism of social life! What facility it would afford in resolving the little problems which are daily arising in every household; and in diminishing the friction that is observed in so many homes! Take a single one of the subjects just enumerated. There are few Christian families in which the question of *amusements* does not come up for debate with more or less frequency. The present winter will form no exception to this familiar experience. It is true, we are in the midst of a bloody war. But nations scourged with Divine judgments usually plunge into flagrant excesses. The English Court, then at Oxford, was never more abandoned to drinking, gambling, and licentiousness, than while the Great Plague was desolating London. Indeed, "it was a time (as a contemporary annalist says) when all license in discourse and in actions was spread over the kingdom, to the heart-breaking of many good men, who had terrible apprehensions of the consequence of it." The same thing has usually occurred in time of war. And as History constantly repeats itself, a philosophical observer might be prepared for the revolting spectacle now presented among ourselves. While death and sorrow are flapping their raven wings over the land—the cry of our slain coming up from a hundred battle-fields, and widows and orphans crowding the thoroughfares, our great cities are resigning themselves to frivolity and revelry. Never in peace did they witness such dissipation; never were places of amusement so numerous or so thronged. It is meet, therefore, that families which profess some regard for the word and worship of God, should decide how far their sanction is to be given to these practices. With many persons, considerations of taste, of decorum, of sympathy for the afflicted, of the respect which is due to a severe public calamity, will be decisive. But if you still hesitate about the theatre, the opera, balls, and the like, you may gather some light from the test the apostle has given us, "approved unto God." You will not deny that this is our proper rule. Do not shrink, then, from applying it to these amusements. If you find that they have the sanction of the infallible word; that where it says 'Ye are not of the world,' 'Be not conformed to this world,' it has no reference to such matters as these; and that, in respect to amusements, there need be no difference between the world and the church;—if you can take these things to the throne of grace, and after asking Divine illumination, deliberately conclude that they are "approved of God;"

you will of course fall in with the prevailing current, and drink your fill at these intoxicating fountains. Whether the retrospect will be as grateful as the excitement of the moment, is another question. Meanwhile my errand is fulfilled by merely counselling you to forbear the coveted indulgence, unless you can lay your head upon your pillow, after it is over, with the feeling, "approved unto God."

Let us close by again adverting to the paramount demands of personal religion. '*How can I make the most of life?*' This is, or should be, the question with us all. And it finds its ready answer in the lesson of the text, "approved unto God." Guided by this principle, the opening year would see us engaging in the service of our Master, with new ardor. Its effects would be witnessed in the prevalence of a more elevated tone of piety amongst us; in the diligent culture of the Christian graces; and in more resolute efforts to protect the church from that flood of worldliness which threatens to submerge, not only 'all the high hills that are under the whole heaven,' but the very ark itself. It would tell with power upon the cause of Christian benevolence—greatly augmenting the willing offerings to the Lord's treasury, and thus enlarging the sphere of missionary enterprise at home and abroad. It would develop the sleeping energies of the church, and send fresh laborers into Sunday-Schools, Home-missions, and other fields white to the harvest. It would enkindle a new and just solicitude for the rescue of the unconverted, and arouse ministers and people to greater exertions for their salvation. It would inform and sanctify the spirit of patriotism, and give our country in this time of her deep affliction, a still warmer place in the affections and prayers of God's people. It would help the tempted, the suffering, the bereaved, to acknowledge a Father's hand in their trials, and might even turn their lamentations into thanksgivings.

These, and such as these, are the benign fruits that would flow from the general and hearty adoption of the maxim we have been considering. It were superfluous to say, that He alone whose glory it contemplates, could write it upon our hearts or keep it there. But, assured that He is more willing to do this than we to ask Him, I respectfully and affectionately commend it to you as your rule of life for this new year. Time is swiftly bearing us onward to eternity. We none of us know that we are to witness the return of this anniversary. There are many seats vacant here to-day which were filled a twelvemonth since by those who were then exhorted to take it as their text for the year, "WAITING FOR THE COMING OF THE LORD JESUS CHRIST." And knowing that death must be poising other shafts which are to lay some of us low during this year, I entreat you all, as I would admonish myself, to supplicate the Father of lights, for grace to live, and should He so appoint, for grace to die, by the ordinance of his own blessed word, 'APPROVED UNTO GOD.'

1865.

VIII.

"TO EVERY MAN HIS WORK."

MARK XIII. 34.

Our Saviour is admonishing his disciples of the certainty of his second coming, and the uncertainty of the time when it would take place. He compares Himself in this view to "a man taking a far journey, who left his house and gave authority to his servants, and to every man his work, and commanded the porter to watch." We need not consider this comparison in its details. A single point only demands our attention. On this New-Year's morning you look for me to offer you a text for the opening year. You have just listened to it:—" To every man his work."

Let this be our year text. It will not be difficult to show how well it is suited to this purpose.

The relation of authority and subjection,—this is the prime idea of the passage. We dwell chiefly upon the Son of God as a Saviour; it is natural we should. But He is as much a King as a Saviour. He is the very 'King of kings.' 'By Him kings reign, and princes decree justice.' His kingdom is a universal kingdom. 'All power is given to Him in heaven and in earth.' And in Him all creatures 'live and move, and have their being.' Absolute dominion belongs to Him as the Second Person of the Trinity. But his sovereignty over our race is also exercised in virtue of his Mediatorial character. He received it of the Father as the reward of his sufferings.

The kingdom thus bestowed upon Him is a kingdom of service. It is by no fiction of law that men are styled his 'servants.' They *are* his servants. He is their Lord. He challenges a control over them which is minute, constant, and universal. It embraces every human being. It extends to all their powers, and to every moment of their lives. He requires every one to serve Him, and assigns to each the work he is to do. "To *every* man his work." Language cannot go beyond this. It takes in every sphere of life, every grade of talent, and every variety of gifts.

Few persons believe this. The common feeling is, that Christ controls the prime arrangements of society and great events, that He superintends the affairs of the Church, and the ministrations of persons and classes devoted to the offices of religion, but, beyond this, that He has little to do with the affairs of our globe. The principle tacitly assumed here is of vicious tendency. It would divorce religion from the daily life. It supposes a broad line of separation between the Church and the world, not merely in respect of the spirit that should pervade the Church (which is a Scriptural idea), but in respect of the supremacy of the Lord Jesus Christ. He rules the Church, but not the world; or if the world, not with the absolute sway He exercises over the Church. His own word gives no countenance to this sinister speculation. As long as the Church and the world are intermixed, his jurisdiction cannot be partitioned off in this way. Providence is a chain; to hold one link is to hold all. It is a mirror; to break it in one place is to break it altogether. He who rules the Church must rule the thrones, the cabinets, the armies, of the world. He who appoints ministers to their vocation must appoint statesmen, physicians, husbandmen, mechanics, and all other persons, to theirs.

And these other classes receive their commission precisely as a minister of the Gospel receives his. It is not that his is a spiritual office, and therefore he is to serve Christ in it; and theirs being secular employments, they may serve him or not according to circumstances. Their work and his stand upon a common level. In either case, the obligation is the same to perform it as by Christ's command and for his glory. It is as much the duty of a lawyer to carry into his profession the motives and spirit of true religion, as of a pastor to exemplify a genuine piety in his work. And so of teaching, of ploughing, of buying and selling, and all other occupations. "Whatsoever ye do, do it heartily as to the Lord and not unto men." This is addressed to Christian slaves in bondage to heathen masters. If they were not dispensed from living 'to the Lord,' who may claim exemption?

And herein is the true view of society. Christianity is no disorganizer. It has often been arraigned at Cæsar's bar on charges of sedition and insurrection, but with as little reason as its Divine Founder. We may not deny that it sows the seeds of revolution. But it is such a revolution as the breath of Spring heralds and hastens in the frozen, barren soil. Its gentle influence permeates the whole social fabric, infuses into it the spirit of a new life, and spreads a new aspect over its deformed features. This is not done, however, by taking society to pieces. It is not done by summoning people indiscriminately to what is technically termed a 'religious life,'—meaning thereby a life dedicated to spiritual functions. This would soon bring the world to a pause. We have all seen the evil working of this principle in countries overrun by monasticism. Society has suffered seriously when depleted, even on this limited scale, of its efficient working material. And if the principle were carried out fully, albeit with a purer type of religion than prevails in those countries, it would prove disastrous to the cause of human progress. It is easy to see what would become of a nation made up of ministers, missionaries, colporteurs, and religious fraternities. Such a nation would soon have to be Christianized over again by missionaries from abroad. The arts and occupations which engross men in Christian lands, are the natural fruit of civilization, as they are, in turn, among its chief supports. A tribe of savages has but few wants. The moment they begin to emerge from barbarism, their wants increase, and they go on increasing, with their intelligence and culture. Hence the indispensable necessity for farmers, mechanics, artificers, and tradesmen; for mills, factories, and ships; for schools, presses, and libraries; for legislatures, courts, and all the paraphernalia of government. These are not the mere embellishments of the social state, but part and parcel of the structure. Nor are they necessary to its civil integrity and growth only, but to its spiritual wellbeing also. The Church could not dispense with them. They sustain it, as it sustains them. Severed from the Church, and spurning its divine lessons, they become the implements of social demoralization; while the Church severed from them (as may be seen in mission-churches on pagan ground) is sadly limited in its means of doing good.

The hand of God is to be recognized, then, as well in the general organization of society, as in the formation of the Church. And while He certainly requires that all classes and conditions of men shall do Him service, He does not expect them to do this by relinquishing their proper callings. He rules the world, not by random impulses, but according to a settled plan. This plan contemplates the gradual amelioration of the race, and the ultimate triumph of righteousness and peace. And this again demands some such distribution of men into classes and professions, as that which distinguishes civilization from barbarism. A complex piece of mechanism it is. A careless and even a sagacious observer may see many a cog, and wheel, and lever, of which he cannot divine the use. But He who framed and who guides the mighty enginery, put in nothing superfluous—nothing which is not contributing to the grand result He has in view.

This thought must be kept in mind. It is the best sedative to discontent. The masses everywhere are doomed to a life of toil. If a Providence be excluded, they, inevitably in the arrangements of society, will find food for murmuring. 'Why should the few be rich, and the many poor? Why should I be shut up to this forge, this loom, this last, all my days, while my neighbor can spend his life in reading and travelling? If I must toil, why may it not be in some nobler sphere, better suited to my immortal nature?' These are moanings which well up from the deeps of many hearts. We cannot speak of them now except in the one aspect which links them with our subject.

It need not be denied, that society is sadly disorganized by the presence of sin. No one pretends that all its arrangements are good, absolutely considered; much less that the entire working of the mechanism meets God's approval. But it is, nevertheless, his institution. Its every provision enters into his plan. He assigns to men their several avocations. He appoints some to rule, and some to serve; one to live by his wits, and another to live by his hands; one to drive oxen, and another to lead an army; and so through the whole range of human pursuits. Taking the world as it is, this is in his view the best method of counteracting the effects of the fall, and training the race for their high destiny. The vital thought is, that He orders these various allotments. "To every man his work." Society cannot answer the end for which He designs it, without the co-operation of all these forces, great and small, lowly and lofty. From the king on his throne to the peasant in his hut, from the sage in his library to the untutored factory-boy, He needs them all. He is using them to work out his plan. Each individual has his own mission. No one can fulfil it for him. And it should reconcile him to his task, to feel that it has been laid upon him by One who cannot err, and whose goodness is commensurate with his wisdom. This reflection will impart dignity to the humblest employment, and smooth the roughest path. If we might suppose a cohort of angels to come down to live on the earth, it is certain that one consideration only would enter into their choice of occupations. 'What is the will of God? What wilt Thou have me to do?' This would be the sole inquiry. And, this resolved, all stations would be alike to them. From time to time they *have* visited our world. One of them brings a message to Abraham. Another comes on an errand of mercy to his outcast bond-woman in the wilderness. A third smites Jerusalem with the plague. A fourth announced to Mary the coming Saviour. A fifth troubled, annually, the water of Bethesda. A sixth releases Peter from prison. Can you doubt that if the whole angelic throng had been summoned before the throne, and these several offices laid before them, and the question been asked, Who will go? they would have responded with one voice, 'Send me?' And if the further question had been put to them, one by one, 'On which of these errands wilt thou go?' the instant and unvarying answer would have been, 'Not as I will, but as Thou wilt!' And so, the more we approximate to these holy beings in character, the less will it concern us where we are to go or what we are to do. It will be enough to know that we are in the sphere to which our Master has appointed us, and doing the work He would have us do.

While this is the actual system under which we are living, it is also the best system for us and for the world. It is no less for our present comfort than our future well-being, that our times should be in God's hand. For his character is adorned with every excellence carried up to the highest pitch of perfection. All the virtues meet in Him which can possibly be combined in the person of a Ruler. His eye alone can look over the whole field, and see what each part may require, and it is the only one which can explore the recesses of every heart, and learn its every care, and danger, and want. His is the only arm strong enough to succor his people when in trouble, and defend them against their enemies seen and unseen.

No heart but his is large enough and compassionate enough to receive all their complaints and sympathize in all their sorrows. This may well reconcile them to those social inequalities of which we have been speaking, and which are so often a source of repining. He is conducting the vast and complicated affairs of his government, as an undivided and accordant whole. To our eyes it may have as little unity, as the driving masses of clouds with which a hurricane overspreads the heavens. But to Him who sits upon his throne in the calm serenity of the upper skies, all is lucid and harmonious; and every creature, and every event, is helping on the final consummation. In such a scheme, it is unavoidable that some should have a better lot than others: that many should toil all their days at the rough work of life; and many make their way to the heavenly city slowly and painfully along the rugged paths of misfortune and poverty. Their agency can no more be dispensed with, than that of the more favored ones (as we style them) who are born to wealth and power. Their comfort is, that they are all serving a common Master who assigns 'to every man his work;' that this arrangement is deemed by Him to be essential to the ultimate and highest good of all concerned; and that He will amply compensate these inequalities in the life to come.

From the principle we have been illustrating, that Christ assigns 'to every man his work,' it follows that we should all endeavor to find out what work He has appointed to us. In numerous instances this question will be of easy solution, for there seems, in fact, little room for choice. Circumstances over which we have no control decide the point for us; and we take a certain path simply because we can take no other. In these cases we may feel tolerably sure we are following the design of our 'Great Taskmaster;' since it is through his providence, as well as by his word, that He is accustomed to make his will known.

In another class of examples He decides the question by the bias He impresses upon the mind, and the endowments He confers. The records of every profession contain the names of men who must have done the greatest violence to nature to be anything but what they were. That Galen must be a physician, that Raphael must be a painter, and Beethoven a musician, and Canova a sculptor, and Milton a poet, and Howard a philanthropist, and Marshall a jurist, and Addison Alexander a linguist, was settled from the dawn of their intellectual powers. We may say, in general, the possession of any endowment is proof that it is to be cultivated; and where, as in the instances just cited, it is paramount and controlling, it may, without much hazard, be held as indicating the 'work' its possessor is to do. In the absence of any strong constitutional predilection, and of circumstances which hedge up every road but one, a true disciple will not ordinarily be left long without some intimation as to the sphere in which he can best serve his Lord. 'Work' of some sort there is for him and for all. "To *every* man his work." As already observed, this allows for no exceptions. To be born into this world is to have a work to do for Him who placed us here. He sanctified this law by his own blessed example. The simple glimpse we have of his early years shows that his youth was given to study and reflection. The language of his townsmen, 'Is not this the carpenter?' warrants the belief that

He may afterward have assisted Joseph at his trade. And from his baptism to his death He 'wrought with labor and travail, night and day,' as no child of Adam ever did before or since. ' It is enough that the disciple be as his Master, and the servant as his Lord.' To say, when summoned to a life of work, " I pray thee have me excused," is all one with asking to be excused from following Christ.

This determines nothing as to the *kind* of work appointed us. It may be any one of a hundred forms of manual industry, or any one of a thousand varieties of intellectual occupation; or any one of a still larger number of passive labors,—the mission of sorrow and suffering. The idea is the same. Life is to be a 'work;' not a dream, not a pastime, not a scene of capricious and fitful activity, not a listless, aimless routine of eating and drinking, and sleeping and waking, but a ' work.' This does not mean 'work' without respite. We have a better Master than that. The service He lays upon his disciples is not the exhausting drudgery of the slave, but the free, loving obedience of a child. It is their right to regale themselves with innocent and timely diversions. Do you suppose Christianity frowns upon all mirth? That it makes wit a sin, and recreation an impiety? If so, why has God made us thus? Has He created these faculties and susceptibilities only that they may be tantalized and thwarted? Or has He formed them to be cultivated and exercised; and so to lend their aid in lightening the burdens of life and fighting its battles? But they must be kept in their place. They are not to be made the business of life, but only its refection; not the end of life, but springs to recruit us on our way thither. This brings them legitimately within the scope of our commission. It incorporates them with the Christian's work. It impresses the King's image and superscription as well upon his mirthful interludes as upon his hours of patient labor and anxious study, while, by invigorating his powers, it enables him to do more work for his Master, and to do it better than he possibly could without this relaxation.

It is very obvious to remark that there are certain qualifications prerequisite if we would do our work properly, irrespective of the calling we may choose. So essential is this that our Saviour includes it in the work itself: "This is the work of God (the work which He enjoins), that ye believe in him whom he hath sent." It is the first step towards working for Him in what we call the business of life. No man can serve his Lord acceptably in any vocation unless he begins here. And this must be understood as implied when we say that a man's profession is often determined by his endowments. A genius for painting, or for mechanics, may justify a man in concluding that Christ has appointed him his work in one of these departments. And he may devote himself to it, and achieve great success. But he will after all fail of doing his work as it should have been done unless he first gives *himself* to the Lord. Nor this alone. The obligation to cultivate personal religion must be recognized as paramount through life. In just so far as this ceases to be the prime aim and interest of the soul, must we come short in the work prescribed to us.

A living faith in Christ being presupposed, our work is to be accepted *as of his appointment*, and to be done *for and in Him.* Here comes the difficulty. How can we go about our daily toil in a religious way? How can we blend our Christianity with all our avocations? This, clearly, is what the text implies, and what a Christian profession involves.

It will manifestly be of great importance to us, to cherish the feeling that it is *Christ's work* we are doing. No matter what the sphere, our commission is from Him. Notice the opening of many of the Apostolic epistles:— "Paul, a servant of Jesus Christ," "a servant of God;" "Simon Peter, a servant and apostle of Jesus Christ;" "James, a servant of God and of the Lord Jesus Christ;" "Jude, the servant of Jesus Christ." This pertains to every Christian: he is 'a servant of Jesus Christ.' His paramount responsibility is to Him. He is as much bound to obey Him, as if he were his only servant. It is of no moment whether other masters or employers come in between himself and Christ. His ultimate allegiance is still the same. And it will not do for him to lose sight of it.

We have already stated this principle and produced the authority upon which it rests. But we may reiterate the sentiment, that it covers the entire field of human activity. It extends as well to the youth who is set to watch a herd of cattle, to the sailor in mid-ocean, to the sorrowful woman turning her spinning-wheel in her lonely attic, to the sempstress plying her weary, incessant needle, as to the Pastor of a congregation, or a Missionary among the heathen. They have their employers: but it is not for them alone they are working. Nor is it merely to earn wages, and make a livelihood. Above all and pervading all motives of this sort, there is a purer and nobler element which, fully admitted, will impart a hallowed savor to their distasteful toil. It is Christ who has given them this work to do. He would not have done it, if it had not been for their good. It may blight some of their early aspirations. It may consign them to obscurity. It may expose them to cruel slights at the hands of those from whom they earn their daily bread. But what of all this, if Christ be satisfied: if He looks upon every hour given to the loom, and the anvil, and the distaff, and the windlass, as devoted to Him; and upon every taunt, and indignity, and wrong, as endured for Him? With this thought, they can do all, and bear all.

A kindred reflection must be clasped with it:—*the sense of Christ's presence.* It is his work we are doing, and He is with us while we are doing it. We are all familiar with the power of such a conviction. Every Christian parent impresses it upon the minds of his children, as one of the daily lessons of the nursery and the family— 'Remember that wherever you go, and whatever you do, God's eye is upon you.' There is not one of these densely populated mills and factories, where the principle is not constantly illustrated. Every artisan, every laborer, has felt the influence of his employer's presence, as he has gone about from room to room, stopping for a moment now at this one's and now at that one's elbow. Every scholar knows how he feels when his teacher comes down amidst the desks and benches, and, drawing near to each pupil in turn, scrutinizes his work and pronounces the due commendation or censure.

Well—the world is but an immense school; and the Great Teacher is always present, by a real ubiquity, with every pupil and at every moment. The world, again, is but a huge workshop. And the great Mechanician, the Author of all science, of all art, and of all skill, is perpetually present,—not going about from one department to another, and pausing for a moment with each craftsman; but making his abode with him, never withdrawing, standing all the while by every operative—master, and journeyman, and apprentice, alike—observing his every motion, hearing his every word, catching his every change of countenance, and even reading every thought of his heart.

Now what we need is to realize this—to feel that the Master is thus with us, noticing our every act, and utterance, and feeling; and seeing how we do the work He has put into our hands. It may aid us in this confessedly difficult attainment, to consider before we begin the day's duties that we are his servants, and live only to work for Him; and to invoke his special help in our vocation. It will be useful to cherish the thought amidst the cares and conflicts of the day, 'I am not my own, but bought with a price.' It will not be in vain to emulate the example of that great Captain and Ruler, Nehemiah, and send up, even in the busiest hours, ejaculatory cries for help to our ever-watchful and gracious Lord. And this his people may do with the more confidence, *because* it is his work they are doing, and He will deny them no succors which they may need in doing it properly.

In speaking of this union of business and devotion, it has been well said,—" Do as little children do, who with one hand hold fast by their father, and with the other gather hips and haws, or blackberries, along the hedges; so you, gathering and managing with one hand the things of this world, must with the other always hold fast the hand of your Heavenly Father, turning yourself towards Him from time to time, to see if your actions or occupations be pleasing to Him. But above all things take heed, that you never let go his protecting hand, thinking to gather more; for should He forsake you, you will not be able to go a step without falling to the ground."*

This last idea is vital. We must do our work, not only as by Christ's appointment, and with a sense of his presence, but, consciously, *in his strength.* 'Without me, ye can do nothing.' If this was true of the apostles, it must be true of all disciples. The strongest of them are powerless in this work and warfare, except as He sustains them. But through Christ strengthening them, the very feeblest 'can do all things.' And strengthen them He will, if they habitually look to Him for aid.

And now, imperfect as has been this exposition of the subject, I think you will all accept this Scripture as a most appropriate text for the opening year,—"To every man his work." Representing, as you do, numerous professions, and endowed with a large diversity of gifts, it deeply concerns you to remember that "One is your Master, even Christ," and that He has given every one a work to do for Him. Could we take this conviction with us into our several spheres of labor, and cherish it as a principle to live by for the coming twelve-month (or for as much of it as we may be spared to see), it could not fail to redound greatly to our comfort and advantage.

One effect of it, which I have already glanced at, would be, to spread a brighter aspect over the entire business of life. For, assuredly, it would put a new phase

---

* Quoted by Goulburn.

upon your counting-rooms, and your work-shops, and your offices, to feel that they are simply apartments provided by the Universal Proprietor where He is in the habit of coming every day to see you, and to help you in furthering his plans. It would infuse new life into your studies, to think that He is your Teacher. It would rest your weary arm, to know that his eye is watching over you at your work. It would relieve the solitude of your dim-lighted chamber to feel that your best Friend is sitting by you, an invisible but willing guest. We smile at the illusions of those amiable religionists, who imagine their deceased friends to be still living with them, and lay the accustomed cover for them at every meal, and set them a chair at every gathering of the family circle. But it is no phantasy when we claim all this, and more than this, for our FRIEND of friends. We know of a truth that He is wherever his people are—whether in palaces or cottages, in the halls of legislation or the halls of science, in the ship tossed upon the billows or the fragile tent quivering in the midnight gale. We are as certain of his presence as we are of our own being. And if we can but clothe this speculative conviction with the warmth and energy of a vital faith, and carry it with us into every walk and every scene of life; if we can enthrone Christ in our homes, our business, our literature, our politics, our toils, our sorrows, and our pleasures, and realize that whatever occupation, or whatever trial, or whatever pastime, demand our care, it is part of the work He has laid upon us, no tongue may attempt to describe the happiness it would bring with it.

This view of life impresses a certain dignity and worth upon every station and every employment, even the lowest. Our merciful Father would not leave servants, not even bondsmen, to suppose that they could do nothing for their Lord; and so they are taught that they are as much included in the rule—" to every man his work"—as the princes and philosophers of the world. Inspired by this sentiment, their hard service becomes instinct with the life that burns and glows in the songs of the seraphim. And so of every service that is rendered, by whatsoever disciple, in the spirit of this Scripture. We have some reason to believe that those of the twelve who had been fishermen did not wholly relinquish their vocation on the ascension of their Lord. We know that St. Paul continued to work at his trade as a tent-maker, after he had entered upon his apostolic mission. Can we doubt that their tent-making and fishing, as pertaining to the 'work' their Master had given them, were just as acceptable to Him as their miracles and their preaching?

And starting here, we may go up through all the gradations of society till we reach the loftiest spheres of statesmanship and of scientific research, and say that as they are 'all under law to Christ,' so, when pervaded by the spirit of our text, they will all yield Him a revenue of praise.

What we need is to be imbued with this spirit. We must feel that our work as it is *from* him, so it is to be *for* him and *in* him. Not only our manufacturing and our trafficking, but the quiet routine of household cares, our reading, our visiting, our travelling, our mourning, our suffering, the duties we owe to our government and our country, no less than those we owe to the Church, all must be put under the guardianship of this divine principle, and linked with the sacred name of Christ.

And if these interests are to be cared for with a jealous eye, as part of the work He has assigned to us, much more must we do what we can, and all we can, to build up his kingdom and save the perishing. In offering you an inspired motto for the year, I have deemed it proper to unfold it in its general aspect, and to point out its just adaptation to human life in its every form and circumstance. As the greater includes the less, the obligation to promote, in every suitable way, the conversion of sinners and the edification of believers,—to promote the cause of Christ at home and abroad,—has been tacitly recognized in the whole argument. But it may be allowed me, in a closing word, to say, that while He assigns this work to one man, and to another that, here is a work which He commits to all. It is the work which brought Him down to our world, which reconciled him to the garden and the cross, and which He is now wielding the resources of the universe to carry forward to its glorious result. He allows us the priceless privilege of co-operating with Him. He stoops to use our poor services in rescuing our fellow-sinners, and ministering the ineffable blessings of his truth and grace to his suffering children. We may not decline the proffered honor. Let us gratefully accept it. Let us dedicate this year to offices of Christian love and pity, to service and sacrifice for the good of souls in the name of a risen Saviour. 'Be instant in season, out of season.' 'Whatsoever thy hand findeth to do, do it with thy might.' 'Let us not be weary in well-doing, for in due season we shall reap if we faint not.' 'In the morning sow thy seed, and in the evening withhold not thine hand; for thou knowest not whether shall prosper, either this or that, or whether they shall both be alike good.'

"Sow ye beside all waters,
  Where the dew of heaven may fall;
Ye shall reap if ye be not weary,
  For the Spirit breathes o'er all.
Sow, though the thorns may wound thee:
  One wore the thorns for thee;
And though the cold world scorn thee,
  Patient and hopeful be.
Sow ye beside all waters,
  With a blessing and a prayer;
Name Him whose hand upholds us,
  And sow thou everywhere.

"Sow, though the rock repel thee,
  In its cold and sterile pride;
Some cleft there may be riven,
  Where the little seed may hide.
Fear not, for some will flourish,
  And though the tares abound,
Like the willows by the waters
  Will the scattered grain be found.
Work while the daylight lasteth,
  Ere the shades of night come on;
Ere the Lord of the vineyard cometh,
  And the laborer's work is done.

"Work in the wild waste places,
  Though none thy love may own;
God guides the down of the thistle,
  The wandering wind hath sown.
Will Jesus chide thy weakness,
  Or call thy labor vain?
The word that for Him thou bearest
  Shall return to Him again.
On! with thine heart in heaven,
  Thy strength in thy Master's might,
Till the wild waste places blossom
  In the warmth of a Saviour's light.

"Watch not the clouds above thee,
    Let the whirlwind round thee sweep;
God may the seed-time give thee,
    But another's hand may reap.
Have faith, though ne'er beholding
    The seed burst from its tomb:—
Thou know'st not which may perish,
    Or what be spared to bloom.
Room on the narrowest ridges
    The ripened grain will find,
That the Lord of the harvest coming,
    In the harvest sheaves may bind."

1866.

IX.

"THIS IS NOT YOUR REST."

MICAH ii. 10.

Having in view the various passages of Scripture which have already been offered to you as "Year-texts," I find nothing more appropriate for the present anniversary than the statement, "This is not your rest." It is so concise as to be easily remembered, so simple as to carry with it its own exposition, and so practical as to admit of a ready application to all the current experiences of life.

As it stands in the book of the prophet, it is part of an admonition or command to the chosen race. They had fallen from their high estate. Their land was filled with iniquity. Yet they fondly imagined they would be allowed to retain possession of it. Palestine had been given them in solemn covenant as a perpetual inheritance, and could not be wrested from them. Their offended God dispels this illusion. He gives them to understand that the country had been made over to them only upon condition of their fidelity to Him. This condition they had violated, and thereby forfeited the grant. "Arise ye, and depart; for this is not your rest." They must relinquish their land;—they would, in fact, be driven from it, and others would enter in and dwell there.

We are not now concerned with these transactions. But we are deeply interested in the language addressed to that people,—" this is not your rest." It has a lesson for us all—a lesson which we shall be likely to need on every day of this opening year.

Besides what the words express, there are two things they imply. First, that we shall *require* a rest; and secondly, that there is *somewhere* a rest for us. On each of these points the Scriptures are, elsewhere, very explicit. Nor could the prophet have meant less when he said (if we be warranted at all in thus generalizing the sentiment) " this is not your rest." Why speak to us of a 'rest' unless we require one? And if '*this*' be not the rest provided for us, where is it? The latter of these topics may be noticed by and by: the former will interweave itself with the whole discussion of the subject. For the present, let us consider how we may take this text as our motto and carry it, to some good purpose, into the scenes and avocations of the opening year. We shall find, I think, that it is equally good for joy and for sorrow, for adversity and for prosperity.

We may begin with the brighter side of life. It may not at first strike you so, but the prosperous, equally with the afflicted, need the lesson, " this is not your rest." Look around, and see if it be not so. Go into these homes of health and plenty, these mills and warehouses into which wealth pours its abundance. What is the reigning spirit there? Allowing for exceptions, is it not, ' I shall die in my rest; and I shall multiply my days as the sand'? 'Soul, thou hast much goods laid up for many years; eat, drink, and be merry.' The tendency is always in this direction. Where the result is otherwise, it is because the tide has been turned back by a stronger counter-current from without. The aspect of society shows how faint the power of resistance is to this pernicious influence. That it should sweep away the crowds who avowedly live for this world, is a thing of course. They yield to it of choice. It is the only happiness they know, and they have no sense of accountability which interferes with it. But to estimate the force of this noxious agency we must come into the Church. See how often it bears down the props and safeguards of a Christian profession. Where will you go, that you do not find a multitude of people who sit down at the Lord's Table on the Sabbath, running into every species of diversion, not excluding the most extravagant, during the week? Where will you go, that you do not meet individuals, once active in the church, whose piety prosperity has blighted as a frost withers a bed of flowers?

Does this prove that the acquisition of wealth is an essential evil? or that it is wrong to desire prosperity? By no means: within due limitations and in the use of legitimate means, there can be no sin in the case. But it does prove that it is a perilous path to walk in; an atmosphere which one must not breathe without using every precaution against the subtle principle that infects it. And therefore it is that this Scripture is tendered you as some slight protection against the dangers of the way. It need not and should not be an ungracious memento—a spectre to frighten you—a pall thrown over your innocent festivities. Why should it impair the enjoyment of life, to be reminded of our actual condition here; to keep in view the important truth (which no indifference of ours can make other than a truth) that we are here only as sojourners in a strange land? If we cannot hear this lesson, there must be something seriously wrong in our characters or employments. And all the more do we need it because it is unwelcome. This is one of the cases where antipathy to the remedy proves the malignity of the disease.

Nor let it be supposed that the admonition here set forth is needed only by those who are thoroughly immersed in plans of sudden wealth, or in gay amusements. Your tastes may run in other channels; they may be wiser and nobler. You find your happiness among your books and your paintings. Surrounded by a few choice friends, you readily surrender to others the frivolities of society, the strifes of politics, and the contests and rewards which divide the great body even of able and cultivated men. This is well as far as it goes. But, even in this tranquil and elevated sphere you may forget the true ends of life. It may be very needful that as you sit in your well-stocked library, or loiter through your choice gallery, you should recall now and then the monitory sentence, "this is not your rest." Peradventure, the occasion for this may be quite as urgent with you as with any of the eager crowd who jostle each other along the thoroughfares of traffic. For these quiet tastes are eminently fascinating. Few persons indulge them without becoming enthusiasts. And an obvious reason for this is, that the pleasure they yield is more satisfying than that supplied by most other pursuits. It comes nearer to filling the capacities of the soul,—not that it does fill them. When was a scholar, a painter, a sculptor, or a musician, perfectly satisfied? But, as among the customary avocations of men, the inherent craving of the mind after some real good is at least better met in these directions than in others. And thus they usually become supreme and controlling. Unless carefully watched, they detach the affections from their true object, indispose to serious thought, create a distaste for religious meditation, and repress all sympathy with the sanctuary, the study of the Scriptures, and private devotion. Assuredly, then, the class of men here intended require to have the lesson kept constantly before them, "this is not your rest."

We pass into quite another sphere, where we offer this Scripture as a sedative to *anxious care.*

'Anxious care!' How wide the sweep of these words! Who can reckon the vast concourse they represent? It were easier to compute the hearts which have not some burden than those which have. The burdens, it is true, are sometimes self-imposed. There are persons who are *constitutionally* anxious. They *must* have something to feel distressed about. Their eyes, by some strange malformation, have one lens too many, and it is always a colored one; so that everything is seen in a false light. Have you not met with these unhappy people? Full of misgivings, skilful in detecting the dark side of things, never looking at the sun without seeing the spots, suspicious of a latent Sirocco in the fresh breath of spring, treating good tidings as the proverbial harbinger of bad, and fearing to rejoice in the mercies of to-day, lest some trouble may come to-morrow! Poor, unquiet souls, what a toilsome journey they have of it! The path to the celestial city (and they have many badges which show that they are true pilgrims) is not over-smooth at best, but to them it is *very* rugged. Somehow they are attracted to the rough places. They rather choose them, because when they come to a spot where there are no rocks, and the air is perfumed with flowers, and the living water sparkles in the sunlight, and the melody of the distant harpers seems floating down from the palace of the Great King, they begin to apprehend that they must have wandered out of the road. Nothing will do which savors of *present* enjoyment.

Now it might seem incongruous to come to disciples like these with the admonition, "this is not your rest." For do they not know it already? Is it not this very conviction that is spreading such a sombre hue around them? It is, and it is not, according as the lesson is understood. What *they* gather from the lesson is, that since this world is not designed to be our permanent abode, therefore we are to make ourselves as uncomfortable here as possible. The true use of it is just the opposite of this. "This it not your rest:" therefore do not be surprised at the anomalies and difficulties you encounter. Do not exaggerate them. They are frequent enough and serious enough. But life is not made up of them. The good Master we serve has mercifully mingled them with our lot that they may keep us mindful of the 'rest' that awaits us, and help to discipline us for it. But we miss the benefit of them whenever we become blind to the mercies with which He has attempered them. Although our "rest" is not here, yet have we resting-places here. There is many a green pasture, and many a spring by the roadside, for the refreshment of weary pilgrims.

> The hill of Zion yields
> A thousand sacred sweets
> Before we reach the heavenly fields,
> Or walk the golden streets.

And if this be not enough to check the risings of morbid feeling, it might surely suffice you to remember what lies beyond the flood. That you have a 'rest' there you do not question. Why not, then, make the best of the inconveniences of the way? Why live in constant fearfulness, when you might trust a Father's care and be at peace? Have you ever found that the nervous apprehension of trouble, as a cherished habit of mind, gives you strength for present duty, or fosters your meetness for the heavenly rest?

But there are modes of *anxious care* which cannot be referred to this source. People who are in no way morbid in their feelings, have their anxieties about their children, their business, their domestic concerns; about public affairs, and about the Church. Do we chide this? Do we say—'It is foolish and wrong: you ought to know better?' Not that exactly. For how can we avoid all anxiety about these things? We have too much at stake. Our affections are too deeply enlisted. We have seen too much of the peril that besets all earthly interests to remain quite at ease. This is not what our Heavenly Father asks of us. At least He would not have us impassive and stone-like. It was not for that He endowed us with these ardent passions and tender sympathies. Life fails of its proper discipline when we become petrified, even though we may imagine we are doing God service. But we need not, in eluding one extreme, go to the other. If we must be anxious, let it not run into a consuming anxiety. Let us not treat the source or occasion of it as we might if this world were our permanent abode. Viewed only in this light, there might be cause enough for painful and lasting solicitude. But there is another light to fall upon the scene. "This is not your rest." Does not this relieve the shadows?

Take, for example, matters of public concern. The course of events both with the State and with the Church may fill you with apprehension. There are periods when no friend of the Church or of his race can well avoid this,—certainly there is but one way of counteracting it. Excluding the doctrine of a Providence and a retributive hereafter, nothing could reconcile one to the moral chaos which the world presents to the eye. When we think what it *might* be and what it *is;* when we compare its governments and peoples in their actual condition with the state they are capable of attaining; when we contrast the relative prevalence throughout the globe of piety, justice, benevolence, and content, on the one hand, and ignorance, oppression, superstition, violence, and suffering, on the other; it is natural to anticipate a future which shall enwrap the race in still deeper darkness, and consign them to a more hopeless misery. This, I say, is 'natural.' Looking over the scene from any mere earthly stand-point, we can hardly avoid it. For the enigmas which meet the eye are intractable to any human sagacity. There is only one key to them; and it is our own fault if we have not secured it. "This is not your rest." Here is the solution of this mighty riddle. This disorder and confusion; this reign of passion and cruelty; the triumphs of iniquity over virtue, of might over right; the slow progress of Christianity; the jealousies and divisions in the church,—in a word, the whole tide of events so counter to *our* plans, and apparently so pregnant with evil—why should this fill us with forebodings? Is it not just in keeping with the design of the present dispensation—which is confessedly preparative and transitory,—where nothing is completed, nothing stable, nothing so isolated that you can pass a judgment upon it without knowing all that has gone before and all that is to follow it? If this were intended as your "rest," you might well be appalled. But as it is not, you have your remedy against desponding fears. Whatever untoward aspect the world may wear to the eye of sense, you know whose hand is on the helm, and how able He is to control the winds and the waves, and how certainly He will bring the ark which bears the hopes of a ruined race into the haven of perfect peace. These tempests are only helping it on its way. And it is part of their errand to keep us mindful that we are not to seek our rest here.

It is a slight transition when we pass from the sphere of *anxious care* into that of positive *trials*. A broad sphere it is. Few of us will get through the year without traversing some corner of it. And there may be those here whose paths will take them into its stretches of deepest gloom and danger. In any case, it will prove no bad equipment for the way if we can go forward with the sentiment engraved upon our hearts as with the point of a diamond, "This is not your rest."

We have seen how much the *rich* need this. Nor less, *the poor*. The one class for admonition; the other for encouragement. How benign its aspect towards the toiling millions! How sad that so few of them should open their hearts to its benediction! Shut the Bible, and the poor have a dismal lot. Hard enough it may be at best. But how much harder without the teachings of our Divine religion! Privation, weariness, anxiety, exposure to suffering and to sin, scant comforts, cravings never satisfied, to-day like yesterday, and to-morrow as to-day,—if this be your *all*, you drag a heavy chain. And is it not all, in so far as the world is concerned? Has the world any balm for your wounds, any cordial to recruit your waning strength, any staff you can lean upon? Can it hold out any future good which may compensate the trials of the present scene? We may not deny that it tries to counterwork these evils. It comes to you with its 'pleasures.' It offers you the inebriating cup, and the theatre, and the gambling-table, and a wide range of kindred recreations. With these you are to 'drive dull care away,' and annul the curse of exhausting labor. That multitudes attempt the experiment, is self-evident. And it were uncandid to deny, that with some it is attended with a sort of success. A dear-bought success it is, however. These so-called pleasures are fragile and evanescent. They break down the better principles of the soul. They nourish tastes and habits which turn into gins and snares for the unwatchful feet. They augment the burdens they are invoked to relieve. Where they staunch one wound, they open another. Every hour of 'enjoyment' they supply is followed by a longer period of pain. And the poverty that was barely endurable without them becomes intolerable with them.

How different from man's is God's remedy for these trials! When He would come to our world to rescue us, He takes his place among the poor. From that first

Christmas night, eighteen centuries ago, the paths of poverty have been sanctified, as any path must be which the feet of Jesus have pressed. Then Christ's personal ministry was chiefly among the poor. All the doctrines, precepts, and promises, which fell from his lips and those of his apostles, were replete with comfort for the poor. And as He tenders them other supports, so also He cheers them with that sweet assurance, "This is not your rest." As if He had said, "You are ready to complain of the roughness of the way, of your hard work, and your hard fare, and your incessant struggle with want, and your dread of coming misfortunes. But did not I tread this path? Have not I felt all its thorns? Have I not promised you my sympathy? And do you forget the lesson so often taught, that these trials are but for a moment? In this life you *must* have them. It was never meant that you should find your 'rest' here. But there is a 'rest' awaiting you. Set your affection there. And when you attain it, you will not regret one step of the way which has brought you to it."

With the same wise and gracious forethought does the Master address this lesson to the *sick*, the *bereaved*, and the sorrowing of every class. For real trouble it offers the only adequate consolation, unless we except the love and sympathy of Christ, and the sense of an all-controlling Providence, which are properly ingredients in the same cup of blessing. There are many here who know, and others who will know in the course of another twelve months, what those trials are. The loss of health is a far-reaching affliction, for the shadow it casts is broad enough to cover nearly the whole sphere of life. Happy is the invalid who has learned betimes that this is not his rest. And is it not to instil this very lesson that sickness often comes? And to enforce it that it is frequently prolonged through weary weeks and months? It found you, perhaps, clinging too fondly to earth, laying your plans for a long course of prosperity, and doing just as you might have done if you had really believed that this was your rest. Your health gave way, and you distrusted your plans. Earth began to wear a different face. Its resources failed you when you needed them most. There sprang up in your bosom longings which it could not satisfy. And, looking upward for succor, you yielded yourself to the conviction that your true rest is beyond the grave. Convinced of this, you found that feebleness and suffering became not simply tolerable, and that you could cheerfully accept them with the feeling—

'Glory to thee for strength withheld,
  For want and weakness known,
And the fear that sends me to thy breast
  For what is most my own.'

I rehearse in this a familiar experience, and one that will be many times repeated before all God's people are prepared for their heavenly rest.

And if this be the lesson of sickness, how much more of *death!* Go with me into this mansion, with its windows closed and the crape at the door. Sit down with this group of mourners. Can you take the measurement of this great sorrow, these lacerated affections, these blighted hopes, these pensive memories, these undefined apprehensions, this loneliness, this desolation? Can you interpret it? Not by the methods of any earth-born philosophy. You can neither comprehend nor solace it.

For aught *you* can do these mourners must 'refuse to be comforted,' and weep on. But another voice falls upon their ears,—"this is not your rest." And instantly light begins to irradiate the scene. The heavenly 'rest' is revealed, not in its splendor, but some broken rays come struggling down into this gloom, which are enough to show that even death itself stands at the very portal of life—

> 'The bright beginning of eternal bliss,
> The gleam of coming immortality.'

Other trials there are which find in this lesson their only adequate alleviation. Their need of it is the greater because they fail of the sympathy which waits upon sickness and bereavement. In the class of trials here intended may be embraced the experience of ingratitude and unkindness, calumny, the estrangement of friends, and also the blighting of the affections. These troubles come with an added burden because they are ordinarily borne *alone*. It may be pride, it may be a false delicacy, it may be a morbid love of grief, it may be a simple conviction of duty, but the wounded spirit declines all fellowship in its woe. The sense of wrong is keen and deep-seated, but the world shall not detect it. The quivering shaft may hang infixed in the heart's core, but no friendly hand shall be allowed to 'solicit' it. And so you nerve yourself, as you may, to suffer in silence. Of course the bloom of life is gone with you; and however festive the scene into which you enter, there is no mirth in which you indulge which has not its underflow of wounded feeling, and of conscious discontent with this treacherous world.

Now of what avail were it to come to you and say, 'No strange thing has happened to you. Every one encounters ingratitude. The world is full of envy and uncharitableness. On every side there are people to whom the best sensibilities of the heart are no more than beds of wild flowers are to the huntsman whose horse's hoofs trample them in the mire. Why mind such people? let them say or do what they may!' This kind of remark must be familiar to you. But it does not help you. There is no balm in it for a wounded spirit. Nor is there in anything which the world has to offer. But it is not a bootless errand to come to you and say, "This is not your rest." Your Heavenly Father means that you shall not take it as your rest. And to prevent this He permits these trials to overtake you. He knows the peculiar discipline which every one needs. Why *this* discipline is precisely what *you* require, you may not understand. But there is a reason for it, or it would not have happened. One thing is apparent: it sets your trials in the only light which can repress murmuring or repining. For it reveals God's hand in them, and reminds you that they are simply incidents of a temporary probation, which, rightly improved, will end in a perfect and unchangeable 'rest.' This conviction will take you to the mercy-seat for succor. And while it may not abate your sense of wrong, or your feeling of bitter disappointment, it may do much to inspire you with a patient and even cheerful temper under your injuries.

There is a different sphere into which we may take this Scripture with the certainty of a ready and grateful hearing. The conflict with sorrow and suffering is painful enough, but it is nothing compared with the conflict with *sin*. 'The flesh lusteth against the Spirit, and the Spirit against the flesh.' 'I am carnal, sold under sin.' 'That which I do I allow not: for what I would, that do I not; but what I hate, that do I.' What Christian does not recognize his own experience here? Who does not know the bitterness of this warfare? Who is there that has not his wounds to show? Who has not been so oppressed by it at times as to feel weary of life? Who could endure it were it not for the assurance, "This is not your rest?" Terrible as it is, this conflict will not last always. It may last while life does, but then it ceases. Not till then, for He who calls dead sinners to life wills that they shall learn something of the evil of sin, in order that they may know how to appreciate their redemption. The rougher the journey, the sweeter will be their rest. And so, however they may rise to the loftier acclivities of the way of life, they shall still find the path thick-set with thorns, for they sow them as they go, and they go on sowing them up to the very gates of the celestial city.

Let me illustrate this by the testimony of a most unexceptionable witness. Writing from her couch of weakness and suffering only nine days before her death, that singularly gifted woman, Caroline Fry, says to her friend:—"I shall tell you why I want no time of preparation, often desired by far holier ones than I. It is not because I am so holy, but because I am so sinful. The peculiar character of my religious experience has always been a deep and agonizing sense of sin,—not past, but present sin, the sin of yesterday, of to-day, confessed with anguish hard to be endured, and cries for pardon that could not be unheard. Each day cleansed anew in Jesus' blood, and each day loving more for more forgiven, each day more and more hateful in my own sight, and hopeless of being better, what can I do in death I have not done in life? What do in this week when I am told I cannot live, other than I did last week when I knew it not? Alas, there is but one thing left undone,—to serve Him better, and the death-bed is no place for *that.* Therefore I say, if I am not ready now I shall not be so by delay, so far as I have to do with it. If He has more to do in *me,* that is his part. I need not ask Him to spoil his work by too much haste."*

These touching words will awaken responsive echoes in many a disciplined heart. In this case, the lesson, "this is not your rest," had been well and thoroughly learned. And the saintly sufferer was eager to go to the land which *was* her rest. We are all studying this lesson. And the deeper our experience of the evil of sin, the more earnest will be our aspirations after a full and final discharge from this exhausting warfare.

There are various other aspects in which this Scripture might be set forth as an appropriate year-text. But it is of greater moment to enforce the primary truth it inculcates. How slow of heart we are to apply ourselves to it and to keep it in remembrance, has already been pointed out. The temptation to take this world as our rest has arrayed on its side the decisive bias of our natural appetites, the whole power of sense, the ties of blood, the current of popular example, the countless fascinations of earth, and the remoteness and spirituality of the true rest. The potency of these influences may be seen in the despotism they exert over the mass of men, and still more, in

* Life and Letters, p. 339.

the perpetual struggle they impose upon those who attempt to withstand them. The necessity of resisting them, however, is too obvious to require argument. Reason and piety alike demand it. It is due to God, and to our own souls. There is neither solid peace for us here, nor happiness hereafter, unless we remember "this is not your rest."

What greater mistake can any man make than to substitute the mere vestibule of life for life itself, the journey for the goal, the conflict, with its scant intervals of peace, for the final repose and crown! What grosser indignity can be shown to our Maker than to allow his dominion over us to be usurped by the creature, and to waste upon selfish indulgence the life He has given us to spend in his service! What baser ingratitude to the Saviour than to lavish upon the transitory interests of earth the love and the homage which are his due! All this is involved in taking the world as our rest. Shall we not set out in a new year with a determination to shun this fatal error? The due consideration of that future rest would curb the tendency to rest here. It is a rest which answers all the conditions our circumstances demand,—a rest from sin, from toil, from suffering, from sorrow, from death, from trials of every kind; a rest which embraces absolute purity, perfect bliss, and an everlasting progression of the soul in knowledge and holiness. It is a rest which God has linked with the present life, and which owes some of its sweetest attractions to our experiences here. The one sphere is in order to the other. It would often check the rising murmur, and cheer your saddened heart, to reflect that the sorrows of your present lot are the necessary introduction to a realm which knows no sorrow. It would chasten the ardor with which you pursue the world, as well as moderate the grief of your disappointments, to remember that with the whole world as your dowry you would still be discontented, unless you could secure the future rest.

Here is our mistake,—that we set so lightly by that rest. In theory we profess to believe that our best friends are there, our most valued estates, our truest comforts. How strange, then, that our thoughts should not be there also! An authority we all reverence has said, 'Where your treasure is, there will your hearts be also.' Tested by this rule, is our treasure in heaven or on earth? Alas, we have to confess that we are so much engrossed with the cares, the business, the plans, the possessions, the trials, of earth, that we often seem to lose sight of heaven altogether. Here is one main source of our unhappiness, our unfaithfulness, and our danger. Our earthly blessings fascinate and ensnare us. They make us forget that they are sent only to refresh us on our way to the better country. Overtaken by misfortune or sorrow, we halt at the trouble, unmindful that it brings a gracious message from our Lord to hasten on toward our rest. If we meet with ingratitude or injustice, we think more of the wrong and its authors than of the merciful purpose of Him who would use it as a means of relaxing our hold of earth, and invigorating our faith in his promises. Let the future rest have its due place in our affections, and these annoyances by the way will not greatly disquiet us. Even the graver calamities of life will lose half their severity. The very conflict with sin will become less insupportable. For how slight the loss or discomfort which earth or hell can visit upon one who is fully imbued with the feeling that this is not his rest, and whose thoughts and desires are habitually occupied with the heavenly rest!

Let this be your resource through all the temptations and afflictions of the year. Nor this alone. Take it with you as well into your brighter as your sadder hours. You will need it to detect the snares which health and success spread around your feet. And it will strengthen you alike in your efforts after personal holiness, and in your exertions for the good of others. Some of you are no strangers to such labors. If you are ever tempted to abandon or abridge them, if your toil oppresses and exhausts you, cheer up, faint heart, "this is not your rest." You must needs work hard here; the Master of the vineyard has so appointed. He knows how heavy your task is, and how ready flesh and blood is to sink under it. But He toiled much harder for you. And it is in mercy He permits you to do something for Him. It will not be very much in the end, but He will treat it as if it were. These feeble but grateful efforts will have a glorious recompense in the rest He is preparing for you.

What greater mercy can I desire for you than that you may all have this Scripture written upon your hearts as by the finger of God, "THIS IS NOT YOUR REST." To some of us the lesson will, no doubt, be brought home during the present year, in a manner not to be misunderstood or forgotten:—

"'The cradle and the tomb, alas, so nigh,
To live is scarce distinguished from to die!'"

And death will not pass us *all* by. God grant that we may so live in the faith of his holy word, and with a steadfast trust in the blood of Christ, as those who are humbly and joyfully looking forward to the 'rest which remaineth for the people of God.'

X.

"MY GRACE IS SUFFICIENT FOR THEE."

2 CORINTHIANS xii. 9.

THE speaker, the hearer, the occasion, and the language, all conspire to invest this passage with a peculiar interest. One of the first thoughts suggested by a perusal of the narrative in which it occurs points to the marvellous dealings of God with our Apostle. That such a man should be selected as an apostle seems wonderful. Nor less wonderful the manner of his conversion. And here a fresh marvel presents itself. We have no evidence that Paul ever saw the Saviour prior to the ascension, nor until He appeared to him on his journey to Damascus. Signal as that favor was, it did not exhaust the fulness of privilege which it was his Master's purpose to lavish upon him. He must also be taken to heaven,—he alone of the apostolic college,—distinguished herein even above 'the disciple that Jesus loved.' unless (which is possible) we are to regard the apocalyptic visions of the venerable John as tantamount to a similar rapture. Paul was 'caught up to the third heaven.' Who would not like to know what he saw and heard there! But he was not allowed to tell. This only we know, that such 'abundant revelations' were given him as to imperil even *his* humility. His faithful and loving Master saw the danger, and interposed to avert it. 'Lest I should be exalted above measure.' What an ingenuousness there is in this confession! It is from the lips of a man honored as no other man has been since. He knew that it would be read by millions. But this shall not restrain him from putting it on record that there was pride still lurking in his heart,—so much of it, indeed, as to demand a stern and painful discipline to hold it in check. "There was given to me a thorn in the flesh, the messenger of Satan to buffet me." What this infliction was precisely, we do not know. Nor would it comport with the design of the present service to consume time with a recital of the numerous conjectures on the subject which have been thrown out by writers of every age and country. Enough that it was some bodily disease, or blemish, or privation, which was attended with suffering, and probably exposed him to derision. How serious a trouble it was, appears from his extreme solicitude to be relieved of it. "I besought the Lord thrice that it might depart from me." "Thrice:" perhaps a definite for an indefinite number: as we say, "A hundred times over I have asked for it." So he prayed, and ceased not, that the thorn might be removed. But it was not. Something better happened instead. "My grace is sufficient for thee: for my strength is made perfect in weakness." 'My strength is illustrated in the weakness of my people; the greater their helplessness, the more conspicuously does my power shine forth in sustaining them.' This more than satisfied him. He was no longer restive under the galling yoke. Rather did he cling to it. He was now as much bent upon keeping it as he had before been upon getting rid of it. The gracious answer of his Lord had thrown a new aspect over his trial. It came upon him as a fresh inspiration, that this implication *might* be made subservient even to his Master's honor. The bare hint of such a thought was enough for a man whose whole being was absorbed with love to Christ. Passing by an instant transition to the opposite extreme, in place of the importunate 'Take it away!' he exclaims, 'I glory in it! I take pleasure in it, and in every type of suffering and shame it may bring with it!' For not less than this is bound up in the noble confession:—' Most gladly, therefore, will I rather glory in my infirmities, that the power of Christ may rest upon me. Therefore I take pleasure in infirmities, in reproaches, in necessities, in persecutions, in distresses for Christ's sake; for when I am weak, then am I strong.'

The petition and the promise, it will be observed, both point us to Christ. 'I besought the *Lord*.' Not only is this the usual title of the Saviour in the New Testament, but its import is fixed by the apostle's own comment, ' that the power of *Christ* may rest upon me.' It is, then, a decisive instance of prayer addressed to Christ; of prayer less imposing than the dying invocation of St. Stephen, ' Lord Jesus, receive my spirit!' but not less significant. The response, of course, is from Christ: " My grace is sufficient for thee!" The word ' grace' here may have its ordinary meaning of favor or love. It may denote the aid of the Holy Spirit; or it may comprehend *all* the succors which St. Paul might need. Differing in form, these interpretations are virtually one. There can be no question as to the real import of the expression, nor any as to the fidelity with which the promise was fulfilled. The transaction occurred some twenty-two — possibly twenty-five — years before the Apostle's death. We are safe in saying that no other ministry of twenty-two years ever comprised a greater amount and variety of labors, together with a greater amount and variety of trials. In the Acts and Epistles we have some notes of his distant and toilsome missionary journeys, his exposures, his persecutions, his conflicts, and his triumphs. No other man has left such a record. But we search it in vain for any intimation that the pledge given him by his and our Lord was not redeemed to the very letter. Alike in addressing the scoffing Jews of Antioch, the idolators of Ephesus, the false teachers of Corinth, and the sages of Athens; in the prison of Philippi, when pleading before Agrippa, amidst the perils of shipwreck, and on his arraignment before Nero, he found the promise surer than a perennial spring in the desert,—'My grace is sufficient for thee!' Whatever friends might desert him in his hours of extremity, there was one Friend who stuck closer to him than a brother. Whatever comforts he might miss, he never lacked the sympathy of Christ. In this he found his rest, his strength, his perpetual reward. As the eye of his Master was constantly upon him, and his arm ever around him, so was the servant's life bound up in his Lord's. He could say, without a figure, 'To me to live is Christ.' 'Not I, but Christ liveth in me.' His affection for Christ had in it something—I will not say romantic, but surpassing in fervor and tenderness that most powerful human emotion which poets and novelists love to portray. It was, indeed, the one sentiment of his soul,—the master passion which subjugated to itself all his faculties, and constituted the centre around which his entire being revolved. He had had 'much forgiven,' and he 'loved much,' as he was much loved of the Master. The double proof of this is before us;—first, in that sooner than have so choice a vessel sullied with pride, Jesus would send upon him a sore calamity to keep him humble; and secondly, in that having laid this additional burden upon him, He assured him that neither this nor any other burden should ever crush him, for "My grace is sufficient for thee."

It is our ineffable comfort to know that promises of this kind, made to individual believers, are the common heritage of all true disciples. And standing where we do to-day, no records could be more grateful to you. You look to me on this anniversary to propose to you a Year-text. Some brief Scripture, which the memory will readily carry, and which may be to you a staff to lean upon, as you traverse the yet unknown paths of this opening year. What better service could I render you than to offer you this precious, comprehensive statement, "My grace is sufficient for thee."

'*My* grace!'—there is more in this brief expression than meets the eye. Here is a promise which runs through all time. It is addressed to many millions of people. It comprehends all the possible exigencies which can occur in their diversified experience. It necessarily implies the control of all creatures and events. It sweeps through the whole domain of Providence. It takes hold upon the vast issues of eternity. Can we refer such a promise to any finite being? Can we conceive of a *creature* as being all this to his fellow-creatures? as clothed with functions which savor so much of the Divine that, if they be not Divine, it would baffle our sagacity to name functions which *would* bear the impress of Divinity?

Consider, in this connection, the force of the personal pronoun here: "My grace is sufficient for *thee*." 'For thee, Paul.' Is this the meaning? Yes, in part; but in very small part. What He was to Paul He is to every disciple. The promise is for the Church universal. It is for each particular Church. But it is no less personal and private. The covenant of redemption embraces the whole aggregate of his chosen ones,—'ten thousand times ten thousand, and thousands of thousands.' But it does this only in virtue, or through the medium, of their individual union with Christ. Often has the thought arisen in the minds of desponding Christians, 'What if *I* should be overlooked? How can One who has a myriad of interests to care for concern Himself about *me?*' But this is unbelief. If these myriad cases were *myriadized* it could occasion Him no perturbation. What could distract the mind of Him who is " over all, God blessed forever ?" "Lift up your eyes on high, and behold who hath created these things, that bringeth out their host by number; he calleth them all by names by the greatness of his might, for that he is strong in power; not one faileth." Sooner could He forget the 'name' of one of these stars than forget thy name; sooner withdraw his care from one of them than from thee. Not only is the Church graven upon the palms of his hands, but so are the names of every one of its members. *Thou* wast given to Him of the Father 'before the world was.' It was for *thee* He stooped to be born of Mary; for *thee* He spent thirty-three weary years in our world; for *thee* He suffered and died, was buried, and rose again, and ascended to the right hand of the Father. Dost *thou* forget that which has cost thee time and money, toil, privation, and suffering? Thou hast cost Jesus of Nazareth too much for Him ever to forget thee. And thou needest not fear, thou doubting soul, humbly to appropriate to thyself the sweet assurance, "My grace is sufficient for thee."

This view indicates, as already hinted, the amplitude of Christ's resources. It speaks of power—infinite power. But not of power only. The word He uses is 'grace.' And this savors of love. 'My love is sufficient for thee.' Why? Because it is the love of One whose character is infinitely lovely, whose wisdom is commensurate with his love, and who has the universe at his disposal. The love of such a being carries every blessing with it. It gives a new relish to every mercy. It takes the sting out of adversity. It makes the roughest paths smooth. It supplies an unfailing resource when every earthly prop gives way, and all earthly streams are dried up.

But this is too general. My grateful errand to you at present is to show you what a treasure you have in this text, if you will take it with you through the year. The bare statement of my thesis brings, as to some among you, instant occasion for it. For are there not those here whom the new year finds restless and anxious about the future? You are shrinking from the possibilities of this year. In the distance you think you descry reverses which may imperil your support. Or, there are tokens of a latent disease, in your own case, or that of some one very near to you, which *may* prelude affliction. Or, the aspect of public affairs fills you with solicitude. On this last point grave apprehension may well be felt. For without discussing this or that scheme of prophecy, all schools are agreed that we are approaching an era of momentous events, and more or less agreed as to what some of those events are likely to be. These conclusions are not of to-day. They have been floating down the current of prophetical interpretation for two or three centuries,—not losing, but gaining upon the confidence of the Church. With these intimations various signs in our own country and in Europe so clearly coalesce, that the expectation of great and early changes in the state of the world prevails even among men who never open the Bible. In this aspect of affairs, as in those also which seem to cast a shade over your own personal future, some relief may be found in the promise, 'My grace is sufficient for thee.' For it is a part of the help He ministers to his people to bid them leave the future in his hands. This we *must* do; for no skill of ours can penetrate the darkness which hides it from us, much less alter in the slightest the channel through which it is to flow. Our duty, then, as it should be our pleasure, is, calmly to await the course of events, without yielding either to presumption or despondency. 'Sufficient unto the day is the evil thereof.' Very sore 'the evil' may be when it comes. But it cannot outmatch your antidote: "My grace is sufficient for thee." If '*sufficient*,' that covers all.

I have spoken of those who may require the aid of this promise even to-day to calm their anxieties as to the future. But, indeed, their case is not singular. We *all* need the promise, and we shall need it from day to day throughout the year. Not all in the same form of relief or succor, but all in some form. Not all, as regards the same office or function of the Divine Promiser, but all in some one or more of his offices.

Take, for instance, that character so often challenged by and for Him in the New Testament: "I am *the Light of the world.*" This, like every other distinction claimed for Him, has its corresponding occasion or necessity in our condition. If He is the 'light of the world,' the world must be in darkness. If He is 'the Truth,' we are in ignorance and error until we are taught of Him. If He is 'the wisdom of God,' our own wisdom is folly. We have proved all this. Is there any one here who has not learned that he is short-sighted and prone to err? Are we not, the shrewdest of us, confounded by questions which arise out of the most common-place transactions? Are you not frequently brought to a pause in your business, in your friendships, even in the microcosm of home, where you reign supreme? Does not the question spring up of a sudden, and confront and disconcert you? 'What am I to do now?' And especially in framing plans which stretch far into the future, and involve precious interests, are you not sometimes oppressed with a painful sense of your insufficiency which makes you cast around on every side for counsel? This promise, then, is what *you* need, 'My grace is sufficient for thee.' It comes from the lips of the only infallible teacher. It is from Him who 'is Light, and in whom is no darkness at all.' In your perplexity He proffers you his friendly illumination. If you will trust in Him He pledges it to you. The problem which baffles you is simple enough to Him. The subject which looms up before you, confused, misshapen, intractable, lies before his eye like a landscape under a cloudless sky. He reads the answer to the question which agitates you, as if it were written upon the starry heavens. He sees the path you ought to take, as He sees the shining galleries along the firmament. He can make them as plain to *you*. His grace is sufficient to this end. And, confiding in Him, you will not seek it in vain.

Still contemplating Him in the same character, let us advert to another sphere in which this promise may avail to our relief. If we need his guidance in the ordinary affairs of life, much more in the quest after moral and religious truth. The helps we enjoy for studies of this kind have been largely augmented of late years, but they are not in advance of the exigencies of the times. The controversy between faith and skepticism,—the 'conflict of the ages,' shifts its terms and positions, its alliances and implements, but it never intermits. The aspect it has assumed in our day is attracting towards it very much of the erudition and culture of the world. It is pre-eminently an age of intellectual activity,—without a parallel, indeed, in the Christian centuries, except in the revival of learning after the crusades, and the waking up of Europe at the Reformation. Not to refer to other departments, the physical sciences have enlisted in their service an army of such workers as were never engaged in kindred pursuits before. Nature is allowed no rest. She is pursued through the heavens and the earth—into the bowels of the earth, into her most intricate forms and shadowy elements, and everywhere she is followed with unfaltering footsteps, and solemnly interrogated, and compelled to surrender her secrets. Amazing it is how many of these secrets she has kept from man for six thousand years. Nor less astonishing how he is, as it were, avenging himself upon her now, in the prodigality with which he is forcing her to disclose them. But the point we are concerned with is this,—the disposition manifested in so many quarters to extort from Nature some testimony which may be used to discredit God's *written* revelation. Not in all quarters. Some of the most profound and successful students of Nature deem it the noblest use they can make of the treasures she has yielded them, to hasten with their gifts, gold, and frankincense, and myrrh, and lay them at the feet of Jesus of Nazareth. Others, however, will have it that the rocks, and the glaciers, and the fossils, and the nebulæ, utter one voice, and Moses, and David, and Paul, and their common Lord and Master, another. And with such assurance are these averments made, that even fair-minded inquirers are sometimes entangled in a network of doubts and misgivings as to the absolute verity of the Christian oracles. There is no proper cause for this solicitude. There is no volume of antiquity the genuineness and authenticity of which are substantiated by so many and such conclusive proofs as the Bible. It is morally impossible, then, that what God has written upon its pages should conflict with what He has written upon the face of nature. Apparent collisions may occur. They have occurred; but only to be reconciled by a more careful scrutiny into the supposed facts of science, or a more thorough insight into the meaning of the sacred text. In this way, it is safe to predict, all seeming discrepancies between the true records will, sooner or later, be disposed of. Meanwhile, we are any of us liable to encounter in our daily readings, in conversation, in popular lectures, assaults upon our faith which we may not be prepared to parry. Nay, the poison of a subtle unbelief may so insinuate itself into your minds as to jeopard for the time your peace and comfort. But be of good cheer: you have one reliance which will not betray you, "My grace is sufficient for thee." When you consider that He who utters these words is the Author of nature, that He created and combined all its elements, and moulded its forms, and ordained its laws, and set the mighty mechanism in motion, and sustains and directs the whole from age to age, you may confidently look to Him to preserve you from being ensnared by any part of his own handiwork into the sin of denying or distrusting Him.

There is still another relation in which this promise may be most helpful to us, as emanating from Him who is the 'Light of the world.' Strictly within the field of theology, and in the study of the Scriptures, we may have, we certainly shall have, occasion to invoke superhuman aid. We interpret the Scriptures aright only as we are enlightened by the great Prophet of the Church. It may happen with some of us that we have mistaken the nature and authority of the Bible as the paramount rule of faith and practice. Others may have been educated in some system of error. Others, again, many others, may have permanent or recurring doubts as to particular doctrines, or the mysteries of Providence, while still another class may be painfully exercised as to the question of their own personal affiance upon Jesus Christ. To these, and to *all* who need light, what comfort is there in the promised aid of the Redeemer! He who is Truth itself offers to guide you into the truth. Only go to Him with your scruples and your fears, sit in lowliness at his feet, listen to his voice, and He will make his grace sufficient for you.

In the next place let us glance at this promise, as uttered by the great Keeper of Israel. We shall all need his Divine *teaching* this year; but not that alone. We are as helpless as we are blind. There is no path leading through this world which is not beset with dangers. The whole Christian life is a pilgrimage, a race, a warfare. There is no progress without strenuous effort, no victory without a conflict, no repose without its perils. It might be supposed that prosperity would insure comparative safety. But if there be any class of persons who need a faithful Keeper it is the prosperous. In your health, and wealth, and honors, there lurk the elements of pride, selfishness, and forgetfulness of God. "In my prosperity I said, I shall never be moved." "Soul, thou hast much goods laid up for many years: take thine ease, eat, drink, and be merry." Every one knows how these toils are spread around the seats of affluence and power, and how many fall into them; how many even of the children of the Church. It would almost seem in our day as if the Church were unequal to the conflict with the world. What with the world's frivolities and the world's politics, the freshet has been rising higher and higher, until some faithful but timid disciples have been looking to see the Church floated away bodily upon the broad bosom of the turbulent stream. Just this catastrophe may not occur. But certainly the "world spirit" has flooded the Church far enough to make all who have any real love to the Church anxious as to where it is likely to be left, if the foul waters ever subside. And, as to individuals, there is no security against the surging deluge, but in the protection of Him who bore the ark in safety over the billows. From these, as from all other perils, his arm can defend his people. And it is with these dangers in full view, as He looks adown the vista of this to *us* untried year, He gently says to every disciple here, "My grace is sufficient for thee!"

This promise has a broader sweep as the utterance of our gracious Keeper. There are, as already observed, dangers and difficulties along *every* path. They vary indefinitely in kind, and degree, and origin. They may be personal or official, local or general, temporary or permanent. They may spring chiefly from the world, or chiefly from the arch-adversary, or chiefly from one's own heart. Rather it is from this last source they all derive their main efficiency. There is no Christian here who does not count upon waging this contest during the year, or for as much of the year as his life may be spared. A mighty contest it is—without respite and without end, except as life ends. And it is one in which the words, *wisdom*, *strength*, *fortitude*, *constancy*, have no place, in so far as our own resources are concerned. The wisest are foolish here, and the strongest are weak. The man has not lived, since the Fall, who could cope in his own strength with the adversaries every man has to meet. Adam himself fell before a single one of these adversaries. How can we stand before the three combined?

Just in proportion as we frame a proper estimate of this conflict, shall we appreciate the munificent promise of the Master, "My grace is sufficient for thee." No other being could make such a promise. He alone has the moral right to make it, He alone the capacity to fulfil it. From his lips it covers the ground completely. For He has fought out this fight with sin and Satan, and vanquished them. As before Him they are powerless,—nailed to his cross, and made a spectacle to the world. "Who shall lay anything to the charge of God's elect? It is God that justifieth. Who is he that condemneth? It is Christ that died." This assures the victory He has achieved to all who trust in Him. Satan could as soon triumph over *Him*, as (absolutely and finally) over one of them. His own honor is engaged in the warfare, and it cannot have an adverse issue. It is as well for Himself as for them He has said, "My grace is sufficient for thee."

This insures the specific aids Christ's people may require. It may happen—it must happen—with some of you, my brethren, in the course of this year, that you will have cause to lament the weakness of your faith, the infirmity of your good purposes, the inconstancy of your obedience. You will have your seasons of dejection. The greatness of your conflict will, perhaps, dishearten you. The yearning of your souls will be after a higher sanctification, a closer communion with God, and a more intimate sympathy with all things pure, and holy, and heavenly, while you may seem to yourselves to be only lapsing into deadness and formality. Painful enough is an experience like this. But it has its grateful remedy. This Divine promise comes to you with its healing balm. It bids you look away from those inner chambers of imagery, so 'full of unbelief and sin,' to Him who is able and willing to succor you. 'They that wait upon the Lord shall renew their strength.' These temptations and reverses which buffet you, may, peradventure, be designed, like Paul's thorn in the flesh, to keep you humble. They will certainly deepen your views of the evil of sin, and so prepare you to appreciate the more the love and condescension of the Saviour. In any event, it is to *you* He utters the cheering promise, "My grace is sufficient for thee." And your trustful response will one day be, "The Lord will perfect that which concerneth me: thy mercy, O Lord, endureth forever: forsake not the works of thine own hands."

If it be the Great Teacher and Keeper of Israel, whose voice we are to recognize in these words, we assuredly hear in them the accents of the Friend and Comforter of his people. It was to soothe his faithful servant in his suffering that He gave him the promise. It did soothe him. It made him kiss the rod under which he was smarting. It transformed a desponding disciple into an exulting conqueror. This was but the beginning of sorrows with him. The infliction of that day was the harbinger of a succession of trials, the like of which few men have ever experienced. But he survived them all. This promise, with its inexhaustible fulness of consolation, followed him, and proved 'sufficient' for him. It will be 'sufficient' for *you*. It is mercifully hidden from us what scenes may await us during this year. But the year will inevitably bring its troubles and changes. Outward reverses, sickness, bereavement, these and other trials will do their bidding here. Where, and when, and how, sorrows will come, we may not say. But this we may and must say, the believer has his sure support and refuge, whatever may happen. "My grace is sufficient for thee." What does this import but that "a man shall be as an hiding-place from the wind, and a covert from the tempest; as rivers of water in a dry place, as the shadow of a great rock in a weary land." There are many here who have proved this during the past year,—mourners who must have been crushed by their afflictions, had it not been for the sustaining grace and sympathy of their Lord. What He has been in the past He will be in the future. 'As thy days, so shall thy strength be.'

We may once more listen to this promise in the utterance of the ever-present Helper of his people.

The question with some who are here will be—the question of all should be—*How can I make the most of this new year?* This question will probably borrow some pungency from the reflection that so many years have passed and there has been so little to show for them. Take, for example, the year just closed,—what results can you sum up from your diary, as connected with the *true ends* of life? Meagre enough must such an exhibit be as to some of us, and unsatisfactory as to all. You would fain do better for the future. You would dedicate your powers anew to God. You would live less for this world, and more for the next. And your inquiry is, 'How can I best do this? What field can I till? What sphere of Christian activity is best suited to my capacities and circumstances? How shall I employ my faculties, my time, my accomplishments, my opportunities, so as to do the greatest amount of good to my fellow-creatures?' Most fitting is it to ask these questions to-day. And if you ask them in the right place, and in the right temper, you will not ask in vain. "My grace is sufficient for thee." He will aid you not only in resolving these questions, but in carrying out your purposes. He will teach you how to apply your energies. He will give you prudence, and meekness, and courage, and perseverance. He will bear you over difficulties, and even enable you to 'take pleasure' in them. And thus for one year, if you are spared, you will not have lived in vain.

Here, my brethren, is the path in which it behooves us all to walk. You have been busy of late in framing your plans for 1867. See to it that they are all comprehended in the one grand, pervading, ennobling purpose of living unto "Him who hath loved us." Then may you go forward, leaving yourselves and your all in his hands, and assured that whatever of duty or sacrifice, of pleasure or privation, of joy or sorrow, of life or death, the year may bring with it, the promise cannot fail you, "MY GRACE IS SUFFICIENT FOR THEE!"

1868.

XI.

"I AM WITH THEE."

ISAIAH xli. 10.

Another of our fleeting years is gone,—how swiftly, we know too well. May I not also say, how kindly? Let me borrow, on this point, the language of a note from an honored and cherished friend, received on New Year's morning: "The old year has been a friend, has loaded us with blessings and privileges, and now lies, like an honored, loving parent, expiring in our arms. Shall we, can we, lay it away to sleep, with the generations which have preceded, without emotion? I can almost embody it in personality and weep. 'Sorrowing most of all for the words it speaketh, that we shall see its face no more.'"

Another aspect, doubtless, the vanishing year must have to many of us. Of its countless mercies we can all speak. But how of the return that has been made for them? When an undutiful child looks upon the pallid face of a parent in death, it stings him to the quick. He could defy the living; he cannot contemn the dead. And so the errors and sins we think lightly of at the moment, rising out of the dead past, often fill the soul with sad regrets, peradventure rend it with remorse. It were no grateful office—possibly it might be a helpful one—could we sit down before that 'Book of Remembrance,' where every act, and word, and thought, of every human being is chronicled, and go back, leaf by leaf, over the pages which photograph our own outer and inner being for the past twelve months. Such a review awaits us,—not restricted to one year, but running through all the years of our lives. The anticipation of this may well arouse us to greater watchfulness and fidelity in respect to the future.

But still another reminiscence survives the decay of the past year, as we look over it to-day. The Scripture tendered you on the last New Year's Sunday as your Year-text, was this: "MY GRACE IS SUFFICIENT FOR THEE." Have you not found this a truth? Whatever your experiences of earthly joy or sorrow, however diversified the wants which may have chequered your lot, has He not made his promise good? And are you not here to-day to testify that, through all the year, He has made his grace sufficient for you?

Let this be for our encouragement as we launch forth upon the unknown sea before us. 'Unknown to us:' but there is One to whom it is not unknown,—one eye that scans the opening as it does the finished year; that reads its every incident and result as if already written upon the starry heavens. Nothing can be so desirable to us as a Presence like this. And therefore it is that I offer you, as your text or motto for this year, his gracious promise, "I am with thee." It is addressed primarily to his Church, and with a specific reference to the combinations formed for its destruction. But it is repeated throughout the entire Scriptures in every form, and in respect as well to individual believers as to the Church. So that we have an undoubted warrant for appropriating it as part of the heritage of every child of God.

"I am with thee." In virtue of his Omnipresence He is with every one and in every place,—in heaven, in hell, in the uttermost parts of the sea, in the darkness, in the light. But this is not the idea here. It is a voluntary, designed, and gracious presence. It is true He is with his people as He is with the fields and the rivers, the forests and the mountains; as He is with the fowls of the air and the cattle upon a thousand hills; as He is with the throngs of pagan cities and the wandering tribes of the desert. But He is also with them in a sense with which none of these have any share or sympathy. He is with them as a Friend and Helper, a Redeemer, a Sanctifier, to care for them, to defend them, to comfort them. Not to anticipate our subject, He is with each one of his people in the completeness of his Divinity, in the fulness of his exalted perfections. Here is something that 'passeth knowledge.' We cannot explain it. Except on the highest testimony we could not believe it. But we have such testimony. And now we can no more question it than we can question his being. We are assured by his nature, we are further assured by his word, that He is as truly present in the plenitude of his glorious attributes, with every one of his children as if He had no other charge. It is no small comfort to them to know that 'the *angel* of the Lord encampeth round about them that fear him.' But still more satisfactory is the promise, "I am with thee." For this means infinite wisdom, infinite power, and infinite goodness, as the guard that keep watch and ward over the believer.

One reason why we are slow to credit this, is the endless variety of affairs that claim the constant supervision of the King of kings. We can only look after one thing at a time. It is the infirmity of our nature that if we essay to carry on two parallel trains of thought, or to give our attention simultaneously to two distinct objects, one or the other of them must lose by it. But here is a universe comprising a myriad of worlds, every sphere with its own peculiar tenantry, and all united in subtle and inexplicable relations, the nearest orb with the most remote, the lowest race with the most exalted; and the primal law which underlies the stupendous scheme is, that in these millions of worlds no child can be born, no sparrow can fall, no wind can blow, no flower can bloom, no insect can float through the air, without engaging the distinct cognizance of the Divine Mind. A sovereignty like this awes us. The half-skeptical inquiry *will* rise, 'How can these things be?' And it costs us a struggle to believe that, with such a charge upon his hands, He can bestow more than an occasional glance and a transitory thought upon *us* and *ours*. But this mistrust has its answer in the history of the race, every page of which illustrates as well the actual supervision exercised by the Supreme Being over all affairs, from the greatest to the least, as his special guardianship over his people. No one who has received the 'spirit of adoption' need scruple to accept the assurance to the very letter, "I am with *thee*."

Not only does this carry with it the several perfections of the Deity, but also the various relations He has been pleased to institute between Himself and his people. It is a pledge of his presence with them as their reconciled

God, as their Father, their Redeemer, their Comforter, their Sanctifier. It includes, in a word, whatever may be needful to them, whatever their supreme good may demand. When a child is setting out on a journey, it is enough if his father says to him, "I am going with you." This covers all considerations of expense, of protection, of guidance, and of comfort. How much more where it is God who says, "I am with thee!" Let us weigh this for a little in its adaptation to our present circumstances.

As already observed, we cannot read the future. We know not what a day, much less what a year, may bring forth. No one would be so daring as to undertake to prescribe the course of events with any individual or family here; to predict that this household will have a year of prosperity, and that, a year of calamity, that death will enter this house, and not that, and the like. This were to arrogate the prescience of the Almighty. But we all feel an intuitive conviction that "the thing which hath been is that which shall be;" that these experiences will all find a place somewhere within our limits as a congregation; and that the opening year will witness substantially the same changes here which have marked the progress of every preceding year. We may go one step further. While ignorant of what may await us, we are certain that we shall need the help of this Scripture. We shall all need it. In what specific form you may require it, or I, is not revealed to us. But that occasions for its aid will come to every one of us, occasions, too, of daily recurrence, admits of no debate. And this reflection may teach us how to appreciate a Scripture which will abide with us through the year, and lend us its grateful aid in all possible emergencies.

There are, for example, before us a good many *perplexing questions*. They arise out of the settled routine of domestic life, out of our studies, our business, our pleasures, our plans. Some of them, judging from the past, will be readily disposed of. Others will baffle our sagacity, and may cause prolonged and painful struggles of feeling. This may occur indifferently with matters of private or of public concern. It may be a question touching the health, the education, or the settlement of a child. Or it may have respect to the well-being of the State or the Church. In each of these latter spheres the horizon has a troubled look. In either we may be compelled to say yea or nay, when the consequences to ourselves or others may be very grave. In these, no less than in his personal relations, it behooves a Christian man to 'keep a conscience void of offence.' He may no more yield to his passions in acting for the Church or the country, than he may in redressing his private injuries. He may not go with the popular side merely because it is the strongest. He may not shrink from opposing error or wrong-doing, because it will expose him to reproach. His Master did not; why should he? The single inquiry he has to do with is, "What wilt Thou have me to do?" This point ascertained, he must go forward, even though it be into the Red Sea, or the den of lions. The embarrassment lies in learning the will of God. That we are liable to mistake here, will be readily conceded. We sometimes err, with the deepest solicitude to be right. But certainly it will prove one of our best preservatives from error to have consciously the presence of the "Only-wise God." In our dilemmas we turn instinctively to our friends for counsel, as we should, for they are instruments in the hands of Providence appointed to this very aid. But we need a higher wisdom, and it is promised us, "If any man lack wisdom, let him ask of God, who giveth liberally." Here is the relief secured by the Scripture before us, "I am with thee." Whatever the problem, however tangled the web, however intricate the labyrinth, your resource is at hand and unfailing. No counsellor so wise as He; none so patient, or so indulgent; none so easy of access, or so willing to enter with a genuine sympathy into every question that concerns you. When you find (as you *will* find in the course of this year) your own wisdom baffled, peradventure, even by trivial difficulties, it will cheer you to recall the promise, "I am with thee." "Every one that asketh receiveth." To have a friend endowed with boundless wisdom always at one's side, and always ready to hear and answer our inquiries, seems all that we helpless creatures could desire, and ineffably more than we could have any reason to expect. The habit of going to God in every strait, and of laying before Him every question of duty, is eminently conducive to tranquillity of mind, while it is simply a becoming tribute from man's littleness to the greatness and glory of his Maker. This is *one* use to be made of our Year-text.

Another will be revealed in its adaptation to *the various phases of the spiritual life.*

As regards *temptation*, it has a twofold bearing, each of which is important. Of course this is a thing not to be eluded. There has never been but one Eden without its Serpent, and it was only for a short time he could be kept out of that. Temptation ambushes every path. It lurks in every trial. It nestles in every blessing. It blends with our recreations. It steals into our devotions. It waits upon all ages, sexes, and conditions. You may weaken, but you cannot annihilate it. It will track you through all your rounds. It is thoroughly mixed up with every man's lot, and incorporated with human life in its every make and mould. It will follow you to your work and your play, to the green fields and the broad ocean, to your library and to your cloister, and to *every* place except your grave. How, then, can this text avail us in the presence of temptation? First, in the way of admonition, and, secondly, in the way of succor. "I am with thee." What a depth of meaning in this, "I!" "The high and lofty One that inhabiteth eternity;" "the Lord God Omnipotent," who is "of purer eyes than to look on sin;" who "hateth all workers of iniquity." *He* it is who is "with thee;" who stands silently by while thou art dallying with the tempter, hears thine every word, notes thine every movement, watches the conflict in thy bosom, and records the whole scene in his Book of Remembrance. Is there not something in this thought to impress the mind of a tempted man, something to awaken his conscience, something to hold back his hand from the forbidden fruit?

But this is less than half the truth. When He says, "I am with thee," it savors less of reproof than of succor. He is not with his people at such crises mainly to observe their conduct, but to help them. It is his own promise that He 'will not suffer you to be tempted above that ye are able, but will with the temptation also make a way to escape.' It is an errand of mercy that keeps Him near you,—treading, as you are, a path thick-spread with snares and quicksands, where the surest of foot may slip, and the strongest fall. He would have you lean upon his arm. For "He giveth power to the faint; and to them that have no might He increaseth strength." They who trust in Him, if they fall, shall rise again; and "out of weakness they shall be made strong." "For the Lord knoweth how to deliver the godly out of temptation."

This holds not merely of outward snares, but of all the complexities embraced in the wide range of religious experience. The most arduous, and at the same time the most imperative service laid upon the Christian, is that of 'walking with God,' and growing up into the Divine image. If we consider what God is in his moral excellence, and then what man, even renewed man, is, the idea of any transformation in the character of the latter, which may assimilate him, however remotely, to the likeness of the Deity, seems to become altogether chimerical, especially when viewed in connection with surrounding circumstances. He has his home in a world which is bitterly hostile to the objects most precious to him. Even his ordinary avocations, to which he is shut up by the necessity of his lot, hang their oppressive weights upon his spirit,—a heavy drag-chain that impedes his every step heavenward. This is plain enough in respect to manual labor, with its exacting demands upon time, and muscle, and health. But his noblest studies—those which take him abroad into the region of high art, or the boundless realm of science—are attended no less with unremitting toil and with earthly hindrances, which will seriously obstruct the path to the Holy City. Nay, that part of his nature which retains more of its primeval purity than any other,—the domestic affections, and the sphere in which they bloom, may become occasions of sin, and have often served to allure the soul away from God. Added to this, there is arrayed against him the whole hierarchy of the pit—Lucifer and his angels, seeing themselves unseen, and plying their mighty enginery of mischief with sleepless craft for his destruction. And, worse than all, clothing every other adverse agency with its chief capacity of evil, the unextinguished principle of rebellion in his own breast invites attack from all quarters, colludes with his assailants, opens the doors to any vagrant band of conspirators, and frustrates the best laid schemes of defence. Is it not marvellous that any man should reach the goal? that the colossal task of unearthing the soul, and lifting it up into a nearer and still nearer communion with God, should *ever* be carried forward successfully?

Yet this happens not with one or two individuals, not in exceptional cases here and there, but with multitudes. It is happening all the while. And the phenomenon has its solution in the brief Scripture before us,—"I am with thee." No other explanation is possible, since there is no other power in the universe competent to bring this contest to a triumphant issue. The customary resources of men are of no account here. Wealth, place, genius, learning, experience, are unavailing. But if God be for us, who can be against us?" Without Him, in this encounter the strength of the strongest is as tow in the fire. With Him, "one shall chase a thousand, and two put ten thousand to flight."

Nor is it material in what form the adversary comes. It may be a persistent temptation, addressed to some specific passion or infirmity. It may be an untoward habit which has been nourished by long indulgence. It may be a proud predilection for skeptical speculations. It may be a morbid tendency to religious despondency. It is all one. For the promise, "I am with thee," covers the entire ground. It pledges not only the relief you need, but *all* you need,—all that the case admits of. Whatever the errors, dangers, fears, and conflicts, this year may bring you, let it be graven upon your hearts, that you have in this Scripture an unfailing reliance,—a source of instruction, of wisdom, of strength, of peace, as illimitable as the being of Jehovah, as sure as his word and oath can make it. What justification will any one be able to plead for spiritual torpor or backsliding who bears in his bosom a scroll inscribed with God's own hand, "I am with thee?"

There will be occasion for this Scripture in another field. If we are to need it in resolving questions of duty, and in meeting the exigencies of the Christian warfare, it will certainly be required *in the troubles* of life. 'The troubles of life!' How pregnant the phrase! How wide its sweep! How broad and deep its shadows! Happily for ourselves, the troubles to come are as yet hidden from us. Our ignorance here is our peace. We enjoy to-day, because 'we know not what shall be on the morrow.' But this we know, that 'man is born to trouble;' and somewhere in the future, we must all meet it.

Our ignorance, however, is not quite so absolute as this. There are those who know well that as the experience of yesterday is renewed to-day, so that of to-day will, if they are spared, be renewed to-morrow. With many persons, life is an unvarying toil, a struggle with circumstances, which admits of no respite. The feet which have trod their monotonous round this week will tread it again next week. The hands which are wearied with the needle, or the shuttle, or the types, through the short days of December and January, will be still more wearied in the long, sultry days of July and August. The poor, nervous frame that pants under the exhaustion of the counter or the school, must take up the same burden with every morning's sun, and sink down at night upon the same anxious pillow. All this is foreseen. It may be none the less painful when it comes, but it is anticipated with a confidence which allows no hope of a reprieve.

Other trials will come without the same premonition. Of this kind usually are the reverses which sweep away men's estates. A thriving business is undermined by some worm at the root. A single imprudent venture converts a prosperous house into a heap of ruins. A dishonest agent absorbs and dissipates the earnings of years. A turn of legislation precipitates upon the country the alarm and devastation of a general bankruptcy. Through whatever channel, pecuniary losses will continue to occur. Some families must suffer this year, as some have suffered in every previous year. And however lightly we may speak of this class of trials, as compared with certain others, yet are they very hard to bear,—too hard for our own unaided strength.

So, also, of sickness and bereavement; they come often unheralded. And whether heralded or not, they will come. Some will be sick. Some will die. Some who enter upon this year in hilarity will begin the next in tears. We are not called upon to appropriate these trials,—to say, this or that will be *my* lot. Neither reason nor religion bids us borrow trouble from the future. 'Sufficient unto the day is the evil thereof.' But when it comes, and to whomsoever it comes, there will be needed a more than human arm to lean upon. It will be a privilege to be able in that day to take hold, humbly and trustfully, upon the promise, "I am with thee." This may, possibly, be required in a sense analogous to that already suggested in reference to temptation. The lukewarm disciple, who needs to be held back from *sin* by the intimation that God is with him, may need to be reminded that his *trial* is of God, who means that he shall feel it. For there are, unhappily, many who exhibit great stoicism, or, what is still worse, positive levity under affliction. They are the successors of the generation reproved of old: "Why should ye be stricken any more? Ye will revolt more and more." A grievous thing this is,—a sin of crimson dye. It is bad enough to abuse the mercies of God; still worse to contemn his judgments. There is scarcely a darker portrait of the faithless Hebrews sketched by the prophets than this one:—"Thou hast stricken them, but they have not grieved: thou hast consumed them, but they have refused to receive correction: they have made their faces harder than a rock: they have refused to return." Wherein do *they* differ from that race who pass through scenes of sorrow without being abased and purified? who remain just as proud, or as covetous, or as worldly-minded, as they were before the rod of chastisement was laid upon them? And of what unspeakable importance it is to all who are in peril of this sin to hear God's voice in their trouble, saying, "I am with thee." This dispensation has not come of chance. "Thou shalt consider in thine heart that as a man chasteneth his son, so the Lord thy God chasteneth thee.' 'If ye will not be reformed by me by these things, but will walk contrary unto me, then will I also walk contrary unto you, and will punish you yet seven times for your sins.' Such a contest as this with the Almighty can have but one issue. "Woe to him that striveth with his Maker!"

But let us rather dwell upon the other aspect of our Scripture. There is *no* trial which in our own strength we can bear as trials ought to be borne. Whether it be disease or death, the loss of property, the alienation of friends, the miscarriage of our plans of usefulness, unjust disparagement on the part of those around us, the conflict with inward evil, the depressing effect upon sensitive nerves of unavoidable and constant toil, the dead weight of poverty, or any other trouble, we *must* have help from without, or miss the due improvement of it. Of this help the believer is assured. What would be of more than the pledge, "I am with thee?" This comes from Him who has prescribed or permitted the trial. He might have withheld or averted it. That He did not, shows that He has wise ends to accomplish by it; that, on the whole, He deemed it best for the subject of this discipline that He should be afflicted. For 'He doth not afflict willingly.' It is not 'his good,' but 'our profit' that mingles the cup. And, when mingled, it is his own hand that presses it to the lips of his child. To believe this, to realize it at the time, is to take from the draught its bitterness. Who could not bear trials with resignation if he might only find some palpable token of his Father's presence, and feel a perfect assurance that his wisdom and love are ordering, limiting, and overruling them? It is only unbelief, my brethren, that can deprive you of this consolation. In every experience of loss or pain, of evils felt or feared, which the year may bring with it, you may cherish the same sense of his presence as if the glory of the Lord shone around about you. And it will recruit your wavering faith, and cheer your desponding hearts, and send you on through the gloom with fresh confidence, to take home to your breasts, as you are amply warranted to do, his gracious averment, "I am with thee."

Again, the kingdom of Christ is a kingdom of *service*. The very act of coming to Christ is defined by Himself as a taking on of his yoke. This denotes subjection to his authority, and obedience to his precepts. No true Israelite would have it otherwise. If there are those who value the Church exclusively for its privileges, declining its duties while they lay hold upon its promises, who spurn the cross as resolutely as they grasp at the crown, let them ponder the Master's words to certain of old: "Ye seek me, because ye did eat of the loaves, and were filled." It is not with pretended disciples of this sort that we have to do now, but with those whose professions are intelligent and sincere. To his true followers the question will come up at the opening of a New Year, and it will often recur as the weeks flit by, 'What can I do for Him who has done and suffered everything for me?' It may conduce to the right solution of this question to review the past, and see wherein you might have rendered Him a better service, how you might have applied your resources more widely, or carried into your work a higher conscientiousness and a purer love.

Without disparaging the results actually accomplished,

we must all concede the comparative inefficiency of the Church,—not its absolute inefficiency. For whatever of truth and virtue, and culture and happiness,—in a word, whatever of genuine civilization the world enjoys, has come to it through the agency of the Church,—not to speak of its sublime and beneficent bearings upon the eternal destinies of men. But, as compared with its means and appliances, we cannot affirm that its performance is at all commensurate with its promise. A Divine institution, entrusted with the sacred oracles, the Sponsor of the only true religion, completely equipped by her adorable Founder for her august mission, not only furnished with ample secondary agents and implements, but made the peculiar habitation of the Almighty Spirit, and armed with the powers and terrors of the world to come,—why should not the Church long ago have carried the banner of the cross around the globe, and opened every human habitation to the sweet sunlight of the Gospel? Need this question be answered? Have we not the answer in our own bosoms? Is it not because we and others, who claim a place within its walls,—the thousands or millions who, from age to age, call themselves Christians,—have so little of the 'mind which was in Christ?' Because the tithes are kept back from the sanctuary, and the flame of devotion burns so dimly upon our altars, and the things of earth steal away our affections from God, and the world divides the homage which is due to Him alone? Peradventure this may be felt to-day by many hearts, and there is a waking up to the high responsibilities of the Christian calling, and a yearning after a closer walk with God, and the ingathering of more sheaves into his garner. You would fain learn the Master's will, how you can best honor Him with your property and your talents, what field offers the best scope for one endowed with your gifts and opportunities. Or, if you already have your field, how you can cultivate it more effectively.

It is pleasant to know that all solicitudes of this sort must be acceptable to God. He cannot but regard with a complacent eye every secret meditation, and purpose, and prayer, that looks to a more thorough self-consecration to his service. In all inquiries of this kind, and *a fortiori* in all the efforts they inspire, you may, without hesitation, apropriate the promise, "I am with thee." Your present or prospective task may be very arduous. You may distrust your capacity for it. Your courage may begin to waver, or multiplied hindrances bar the way. Unthought-of difficulties embarrass you. Human sympathy fails you. You are tempted to lay up your pound in the napkin, and keep it there until the Master comes. But this is unbelief. You have forgotten who it is that saith, "I am with thee." Open your heart to this voice from heaven. It never deceived any one. It will not deceive *you*. Let all his professing people set out anew with this sentiment transfused through their hearts, and there will be no ciphers, no loiterers here. Every one will be a worker of some kind, in some field, and all will work with the cheerful tone and temper of children serving a loving Father, whose smile is their encouragement, and whose presence is their delight.

Such, then, is the New Year's gift I offer you,—rather let me say, which He offers you, whose condescending word it is, "I am with thee." Take it with you, my brethren, as you go on your way. Take it to your homes, to your schools, to your shops and your counting-rooms, to your closets, to the sanctuary, into every sphere of duty, into every scene of sickness and of sorrow, into every scene of innocent mirth. 'Bind it for a sign upon your hands, and as a frontlet between your eyes. Write it upon the posts of your houses and upon your gates,' "I am with thee." It will be your light in darkness, your strength in weakness, your shield in danger, your chief joy in prosperity, your comfort in affliction; and, should your pilgrimage close during the year, your solace in death. Through all the changes of this year, in all its experiences, may you, day by day, and hour by hour, have the faith, and the courage, and the patience, and the consolation bound up in this Divine promise, "I AM WITH THEE!"

1870.

XII.

"A LITTLE WHILE."

JOHN xvi. 16.

In the gracious providence of God I am permitted to meet you again on a New Year's Sabbath. Two years ago to-day I addressed you in circumstances which I can never forget; for the service here was followed, within a few hours, by a sudden and dangerous illness that forbade my even looking upon your faces for many months. One year since I was separated from you by more than a thousand miles. So that to be allowed to spend this day with you is a privilege for which I desire to present my earnest thanksgiving to God.

I know not how far these recent experiences may have influenced my selection of a Scripture to offer you this morning. But you will not think it strange that, in the midst of such changes, I should propose to you, as your text for the year, that brief utterance of the Saviour,—"A little while." Brief it is, but what a depth of meaning it embosoms! There are moments in our lives which seem to be hours; hours which might almost pass for years. And thus a volume, yea a great folio, may sometimes be condensed into one or two simple words.

You will recall the connection, and the perplexity of the Twelve on the occasion here referred to, "A little while and ye shall not see me: and again, a little while, and ye shall see me, because I go to the Father." Their imperfect faith could not comprehend this language. Often as He had told them what awaited Him, they could not believe that He was to die. To the very last their thoughts were of an earthly Messiah and a temporal kingdom. Even now, within twelve hours, perhaps, of the crucifixion, they study in vain to affix a definite meaning to his words, and they say among themselves, "We cannot tell what He saith."

Nor can we tell all that this expression may carry with it as to us and ours. Some things there are, however, too patent to be mistaken, the due consideration of which may be helpful to us as we enter upon another year.

In the multiplicity of themes and objects to which this phase may be applied, let us glance briefly at some general views, before bringing the thought directly home to ourselves.

Look, then, at the condition of the world. Eighteen centuries have elapsed since the Son of Man returned to the Father. He came to our globe as the great, the only Renovator, to "make all things new." Whatever amelioration has taken place in the state of mankind is to be traced to his mission. That some nations have emerged from the thick darkness of paganism; that there are countries enriched with the blessings of a true civilization; that millions have been renewed and gathered into the Church of Christ; is wholly owing to the incarnation and death of the Son of God. Let us not be ungrateful for results like these. But no intelligent

Christian can be satisfied with the existing state of things. No one can contemplate it without sadness. The mass of the race still sit in darkness. Where the true God has one even nominal worshipper, five or six embruted mortals kneel before dumb idols. Within the domain of Christendom error and vice run riot. More altars have been reared to philosophic Atheism within the last half century than in any equal period since the Reformation. Unwearied efforts are making to coerce the sciences into a gigantic crusade against revealed religion; and scores of *savants*, rich in university honors, are trying their best to teach creation to blaspheme the Creator. Of the very churches which bear the name of Christ, whole denominations have so perverted and overlaid the ancient faith that it is virtually replaced with "another gospel." Even in the Protestant communions there are well-developed tendencies on the one hand towards Romanism, on the other, towards Rationalism;—Herod and Pilate, burying their mutual hate to cabal together against Jesus of Nazareth.

The picture, it is true, has its brighter side. There are Churches which adhere to the Gospel in its purity. There are tens of thousands of believers who cease not to testify by word and example against the prevalent impiety of the age, and the more pernicious worldliness of the Church. There is a noble army of faithful workers who are toiling at home and abroad, in public and in private spheres, using all legitimate methods and implements, sowing beside all waters, and never wearying in their efforts to save the perishing, and diffuse the blessings of redemption. There are powerful nations even revolting against the Papal despotism, and groping after a purer faith and a truer liberty. It were inexcusable to overlook or disparage this aspect of the times.

But, after all, the most sanguine disciple must admit that Christianity has not made the progress which might naturally have been anticipated for it. Looking abroad upon the hosts of error that are marshalling their forces against it, under so many flags and in so many fields, he may well exclaim, 'How long, O Lord, how long?' It is a timely appeal, and directed to the right quarter. For, however inscrutable to our poor wisdom the course of events upon which we are meditating, we are not for one moment to imagine that He has resigned his sceptre, or that He does not hold this turbulent chaos under his absolute control. "Let the heathen rage." Let false teachers sow tares among the wheat, and false prophets prophecy lies. What then? The Lord of glory still sits as King upon his holy hill of Zion. He will make the wrath of man to praise Him, and the remainder of wrath He will restrain. Let it be for the comfort of his people as they gaze upon this turmoil,—"A little while." Whether it will be literally so, as measured upon our dials, we may not affirm with confidence, albeit this is the conviction of some masters in Israel. But that it will be 'a little while,' as measured by his great cycles, we are positively certain. In his own good time He will come to the succor of his people, and vindicate his own cause against the confederate hosts of earth and hell. What He may permit his adversaries to achieve before He intervenes, is not distinctly revealed to us. But there are intimations in his word that the vast tide of delusion and iniquity has not yet attained its full volume. Paganism was allowed four thousand years to test its capacity for reclaiming and elevating the race. A godless Christianity—that is, human reason, as nurtured and expanded by the institutions of that religion to which, in requital of its fostering care, it would gladly play the assassin, is now essaying the same problem. Among the hosts of authors and philanthropists of the day, there is no class more conspicuous, none certainly more supercilious, than the men who are for reforming the world without the Gospel. If they fail, it will not be from lack of numbers, of learning, of assiduity, or of self-confidence. In these elements they will bear a favorable comparison with any school of reformers the world has ever seen. It would be rash to predict that their assaults upon Christianity will prove absolutely abortive. They have already ensnared many persons of eminent intellectual gifts and of high social position. There is every probability that others will follow. Led by a few names justly distinguished in the walks of science, sustained by an army of smatterers, and encouraged largely by the sympathy of the popular press, it were not strange if they should succeed to some extent in poisoning the public mind against the evangelical faith. Nor is the other wing of this allied force in a less promising way. The Rationalists are assailing the Church from without; the Ritualists are plying their enginery within. Those deal in open attack. These are sappers and miners. Inimical to each other, they are alike hostile to spiritual religion. The final triumph of one party would land the race in bald atheism. That of the other would renew the formalism, the superstition, and the persecutions of the Dark Ages. That each may succeed in a measure is not unlikely. The wisdom of this world, peradventure, must needs have this further trial, that all men may see its impotency in devising any effective remedial system, even when equipped with weapons it has covertly stolen from the armory of Christianity.

For the ultimate result is not doubtful. The humble believer has as little reason to fear for the final safety and triumph of the Church, as Noah and his family had for the safety of the ark. The same sleepless eye that watched over the ark, and the same omnipotent hand that guarded it, are enlisted on behalf of the Church. A barque that has ridden out the storms of sixty centuries, is not going to founder as it nears the port. In '*a little while*' He that shall come, will come and will not tarry. "Strengthen ye the weak hands and confirm the feeble knees. Say to them that are of a fearful heart, Be strong, fear not: Behold, your God will come with vengeance, even God with a recompense: He will come and save you. And the ransomed of the Lord shall return and come to Zion with songs and everlasting joy upon their heads: they shall obtain joy and gladness, and sorrow and sighing shall flee away."

If I have dwelt somewhat upon this topic, it is because there is nothing more prominent in the outlook which greets us at the opening of this year, than the relations of pure Christianity with the numerous bands of errorists who are assailing it on every side, and constantly receiving fresh reinforcements. We may thank God and take courage, when we reflect that this can last only for 'a little while.'

But let us come nearer home. This year-text has its immediate personal lessons for us all—lessons so many and so varied that the only embarrassment lies in deciding what line of illustration to adopt.

One thing is apparent:—if this thought, "a little while," were so incorporated with our being that we could not, without an effort, divest ourselves of it, it would tell with great power upon the issues of this new year. Once, perhaps once only, its full impression has been exemplified. There was an unwearied worker who said, "I must work the works of Him that sent me while it is day; the night cometh when no man can work." With our blessed Master it was always—"a little while." He never lost the feeling, even for a moment. There was no faltering of hands or feet, of heart or tongue. And the results—who shall compute them? Into that one short life were condensed ages upon ages of other lives, whether human or seraphic. Nay, we may not degrade his mission by *any* comparison, save in the way of contrast. In that "little while" of his earthly pilgrimage were bound up issues which demand the universe for their theatre, and eternity for their development.

Yet we may without irreverence claim, that many others have lived measurably under the influence of this feeling; and every one of them has had something to show for life. You will recall examples of this kind which embellish the annals of the various professions and occupations—statesmen, captains, authors, jurists, mechanics, merchants. Wherever we find a man who has taken it for his motto, "a little while," he is certain to bring something to pass—something good or evil. The human mind, even in its lower stages of culture, is a cunning piece of mechanism which cannot be kept in constant and energetic activity without making its power felt somewhere. No petty asteroid can sweep along its orbit without affecting other asteroids, and planets even. And when it comes to the higher sphere of religion and morals, an earnest life can no more fail of yielding fruit than could the trees in the Garden of Eden.

Varying indefinitely as we do in our gifts and advantages, what we lack, any of us, is not so much talents or opportunity, as love, and zeal, and devotion to our work. It is not written, as it should be, in our hearts, and upon the palms of our hands—"a little while." We work, too often, as if life were still measured by centuries. Our years are spent in getting ready to live; and just as the lamp is well filled, and trimmed, and burnished, the glimmering flame that was to have blazed forth its splendors, goes out. It may put us on our guard against this common and fatal mistake to consider, though in two or three particulars only, the work we have to do, and to deduce hence how needful it is that we go about it with the feeling—"a little while."

If I mention *self-culture*, what images of neglect, what hopes and longings, what despondencies and possibilities, rise before the mind. It belongs to the alphabet of our religion, that every talent carries with it its own law of improvement; and that all our gifts and acquisitions are to be dedicated to God. Up to a certain age, we are 'under tutors and governors.' If they and we are true to each other, the process of culture will be well inaugurated. But it is a beginning only. What we technically style 'an education,' is mainly a training of the faculties for their work. That multitudes never get beyond this—come to a stand when dismissed from school or college, and learn, afterwards, only what comes by a sort of absorption in the unavoidable intercourse of society, and the current of events,—is as true as it is humiliating. We all see and deplore their error. Possibly in its extreme type, we elude it. But a narrow census would comprehend those who really make of life all that might and should be made of it.

Many fail from the want of a plan. There is no definite object they propose to themselves: certainly there are no definite methods for attaining it. Working without order or system, their random efforts miscarry because they lack aim and coherence. Something more than strength is needed to wield a sledge to good purpose, even though it be the strength of a Colossus. Just here lies the secret of many a man's failure whose generous gifts gave presage of a brilliant success. The swiftest barque will make a long voyage, or fail of reaching port altogether, if, instead of keeping her course, she suffers the capricious winds to carry her where they choose. It is essential to live for something, to know what that something is, to keep it ever in view, and to select the aptest means for accomplishing it. In each of these particulars we may derive a wholesome stimulus from the thought—"a little while." It would aid us in choosing an object worthy in itself, and suited to our situation and capacities. It would prompt to a prudent husbanding of our resources in the prosecution of the chosen purpose. It would check discursive and impotent labors in pursuit of alien ends. It would enforce the necessity of resolute, efficient working while the day lasts.

'Self-culture,' it need scarcely be observed, comprises the whole man. To speak of the intellectual powers chiefly, how slothful we are, for the most part, in our quest of knowledge! I confess that to sit down in a great library and make a survey of the crowded shelves, is apt to awaken a feeling of despondency. 'Here are ten thousand books I should like to read. Could I live as long as Methusaleh, I might. As it is, a few volumes are all I could compass. I will not give my time to so fruitless a task.' Thus you soliloquize, but not wisely. The craving after knowledge is natural and healthful. And you are right in the assumption that it cannot be satisfied within the brief term of human life. Neither could it have been with the primeval longevity which the sight of a library makes you covet. Were a special dispensation to spare you till you had read all these books, you would only crave more. This is one of the tokens of the soul's immortality—this perpetual yearning after truth which, instead of being sated, only grows by indulgence. It points ever to the future, and will still point to the future when this mortal shall have put on immortality. Does any one doubt that the angels are thirsting for knowledge, as we are?

The inability, then, to master a whole library need not dishearten you. That is not the design of a library. It is simply an Encyclopædia—for reference as to all subjects, for the *study* of a few. Omnivorous reading is no more to be commended than omniverous eating, except in the case of those mental prodigies who do not fall under general rules. The wise student will choose his field or fields of research, and aim rather to explore them thoroughly than to skim over countless parterres. Accepting contributions to his garners from every quarter, and, as far as possible, interrogating every object and every incident, he will still hold to his main purpose, and lay out his strength upon what he has adopted as his lifework. Nor is there any branch of learning which will not furnish ample room for the exertion of all your powers. It is the grand distinction of the Temple of Truth, that you may traverse any one of its galleries and never reach its end: they all stretch off into the infinite. The devotees of the sciences, physical and metaphysical, perceive this, and are beguiled, often, into the error of investing science with the attributes which belong only to a personal, and infinitely wise and great Creator. Taught in a different school, you will recognize alike in the phenomena of nature and in the vast complexities and onward progress of human affairs, the manifestations of the presence and sovereignty of God, the source and centre, the sum and end of all truth. Impressed with this conviction, it will need only the abiding feeling—'a little while,' to lend unity and energy to your studies, as it will also dispose you to bring all your acquisitions and lay them, as the Magi did their gifts, at the Saviour's feet.

If this train of thought concern rather the few than the many, there is one aspect in which it adapts itself to us all. Knowledge of every kind is valuable. But the knowledge of God, of his word, and his redeeming work, is indispensable. The wide diffusion of religious knowledge generally, is one of the honorable distinctions of our times. But has not the current lost somewhat in depth? There are more good books, and more who read them. But has there been a corresponding increase of acquaintance with the Scriptures in the Church? To speak of our own communion only, is the Bible *studied*, relatively, as much as it used to be? Are there as many Christians who attain to an intelligent and discriminating perception of its truth? While there is more Christian activity and discussion abroad, is there as much Christian knowledge?

However these questions may be answered, there is one concession we must all make,—*we know too little of the Bible.* Those who have consciously neglected it, and those who have not neglected it, will unite in this confession. There can be no one here who would not like to know more of this blessed book before he meets face to face that Saviour who is its only theme. The season is one which invites to a freshened ardor in the prosecution of this best of studies. If we are ever to enrich ourselves from this treasury of sacred truth, we must be about it. The penury of our present stores may well humble us. And 'a little while' only is left us in which to augment them. How can we better employ the brief space that may remain to us than in dedicating a considerable portion of it to the diligent and prayerful study of the Scriptures? Whatever be neglected, let us aspire after larger views of the perfections and government of God, of the Mediator and his several offices, and of the gradual unfolding of that wondrous scheme of mercy which, stretching from eternity to eternity, has inscribed on its vast roll all our hopes and interests as individuals, and the destinies of the entire race. Here is a kind of knowledge, the highest and best of all, for the acquisition of which we are not dependent upon costly libraries. We have the text-book, the Book of books, in our hands. Under the illumination of the Divine Spirit, the humblest, alike with the most gifted, may gain access to its inexhaustible treasures, and make them their own.

> " 'Tis a broad land of wealth unknown,
>   Where springs of life arise;
> Seeds of immortal bliss are sown,
>   And hidden glory lies."

In apportioning our "little while" among the numerous objects which solicit attention, can we afford to overlook the field which hides the 'pearl of great price?'

We simply advance a step further in the same direction when we speak of that *inner life* of the believer, the nourishing of which is equally imperative and difficult. There are those to whom the current language of the Scriptures and of Christian people, on the corruption of the heart, seems extravagant, if not fanatical. The reason is obvious. It is a subject about which they are ignorant. Intelligent they may be, skilful in resolving abstruse questions, at home among the rocks, the forests, and the stars, but they are strangers to themselves. They have never seen, have never honestly sought to see, their own hearts. How should they comprehend the depth and force of their evil appetites when they have put forth no resolute effort to subdue them? The Christian knows better. To him the seventh chapter of Romans is neither myth nor fable. In St. Paul's experience he recognizes his own. He is waging the same war with the 'law of sin' in his members, receiving the same wounds, cast down by the same reverses, and cheered by the same triumphs. The heart is as a field overspread with noxious plants rooted so firmly that the weeding of the ground is the labor of a life. Not only so, but it must not be intermitted. In ordinary horticulture it is a needful, but only an occasional, task. Here the tropical fertility of the soil leaves the gardener no respite from labor. The clinging roots baffle his skill, and nothing is more common than to find the pestilent vine which he imagined he had extirpated suddenly shooting forth again with a luxuriant growth.

This conflict pertains to the entire earthly life of the believer. How urgent it is, how incessant, how painful, no disciple requires to be told. Essentially it is the remoulding of the soul. While the works remain the same, without any organic change, they have all to be renovated and readjusted, so that it amounts to a "making all things new." This process may have been commenced with us; but how incomplete it is even where it has advanced the farthest! Who of us could bear the thought of going as we are now into that awful presence where angels veil their faces? Something more we hope to do before that hour comes; something more we feel that we *must* do in the way of crucifying the flesh with its affections and lusts, and putting on Christ. In striving after this result, it cannot fail to be of service to us to keep in mind the thought—"a little while." The student at his task, the pilgrim on his journey, the sailor descrying his haven, the soldier on his march,—this thought is a talisman to them all. Much more should it nerve the spiritual warrior to ever-increasing constancy and courage. You may not suspend your efforts. The rest you long for, you cannot take. Every path you tread is thickly ambushed. Your own bosom is full of spies and traitors. To sleep, or loiter, or put off your armor, or hold parley with the enemy, will involve you in certain loss. But, then, 'the time is short.' The conflict will last while life lasts, but that can be at most for only 'a little while.' And, however subtle and trained the allied forces against you, you meet them with the consciousness of a strength and a sagacity immeasurably superior to their own. For you also have an Ally. He is One who hath his way in the whirlwind and in the storm, and "the clouds are the dust of his feet;" who is "mightier than the noise of many waters; yea, than the mighty waves of the sea." It is his wisdom and his strength you wield. And his word is pledged to you, "No one shall pluck them out of my hand." It were base to retire from such a conflict when you *know* that it must end in 'a little while,' and end in your triumphant and lasting success.

Animating as this may well be to all Christians, there are some to whom it must come with the balm of a signal encouragement. Perhaps the consideration which oftener than any other makes a Christian willing to die, is that upon which we have been dwelling,—this incessant, exhausting fight with his own corruptions. Thrice comforting must this 'little while' be to the various tribes of tempted and desponding disciples. Among them are some whose physical infirmities give a sad coloring to their spiritual life; others who seem to be the special objects of Satanic malignity; and others still who, from some erroneous teaching, from feeble health, from ill-governed affections, or other cause, live, as it were, in a haunted house, beset with visions and imaginings, which supersede the materialism of earth and sense, and create an unreal world, fearful to dwell in, and impossible to escape from. To all these sufferers the text brings its words of solace. Your trials no one can disparage who is conversant with the believer's warfare. They must be ranked as among the most painful allotments which our Heavenly Father permits his children to encounter. But it is through his permission they come. He will limit and control them. In his own good time, which must needs be in "a little while," He will bring them to an end. And then, ye poor, tempted, wearied, but still obedient, trusting, souls, will He 'reward you double' for the sorrows of the way. What will these concern you when once you hear that joyful salutation, "Come, ye blessed of my Father!"

There are other conflicts which require this solace. With a certain class of minds, there is an impatience of our present condition—of the mystery of Providence, and of limits imposed upon our possible knowledge of the unseen and the spiritual, which involves a perpetual inward struggle. You accept the written word as of Divine authority. But it fails to explain the moral chaos to which the world has been consigned for these sixty centuries. Why did the All-wise and All-good suffer the bloom of Eden to be so suddenly blighted? Why permit the fair fabric of creation which He had just pronounced 'Very good,' to be polluted and despoiled by the tempter? Why must sin and death be allowed to ravage the earth for all these ages? Why does the black pall of paganism still rest upon hundreds of millions of the race? Why are other hundreds of millions abandoned to the sway of the Man of Sin and the False Prophet? Why is the Church itself fissured with error and paralyzed with selfishness and formalism? Why that *eternity* of woe which awaits the unbelieving! What and how intricate are the bonds which unite us with other races of beings? How is the soul to subsist when severed from the body, and what scenes are to greet the departing spirit immediately after death? What conceptions are we to form of heaven, and of the employments of the righteous in glory?

Questions like these are ever floating before your minds.

At times they roll in on you in a body for an answer with a vehemence which menaces your moorings. You assail the massive wall which divides between the material and the spiritual, the present and the future, as a bird beats against the bars of its cage,—and to as little purpose. The wall will not yield. A single hand only can raze it; and will not raze it for *you*. So far from it, you are required not only to acquiesce in these arrangements as founded upon adequate reasons, but to believe that they are meant to supply the very training you yourselves need. Herein is the discipline of faith, of patience, of humility, of filial trust. "Except ye become as little children, ye shall not enter into the kingdom of heaven." It was the teaching of the tempter, "Ye shall be as gods." And it might seem as if the fatal promise carried the temper with it: for men have ever since borne themselves "as gods." The true God will not endure this. Instead of "gods," we must be transformed into children, yea, "into *little* children"—guileless, helpless, loving, trustful, obedient, grateful. A tardy process it is, and painful, but it *must* go forward. Our comfort is, that it will be temporary. In "a little while" you will be discharged from this regimen, so trying to flesh and blood; and, still more, relieved of the enigmas and perplexities out of which it springs. The curtain *will* be lifted. The labyrinth you have been traversing all your lives, will end in a large and wealthy place. A flood of light will pour itself over this dimness and seeming disorder which baffle our highest wisdom and ensnare our faith. The paradoxes of time will become the intuitions of eternity, and the mysteries of earth, the hallelujahs of heaven.

I have alluded to the bearing of our text upon the

work of life. The topic, while all-important, is so familiar that we rarely get any just impression of its vast significance. What is it, the work of life? "Man's chief end is to glorify God and enjoy Him forever." Is it not for *this* He made us and placed us here, that we might serve and honor Him? Something, possibly, has been done, or attempted, in that way. But how little have they done, who have done most! And as to the greater part of us, what confusion would cover us should we be called now to his bar, with the meagre showing we might be able to make for our twenty, forty, or fifty years! If reminded that we have only "a little while" for retrieving the past—no, that, alas, can never be done, but for improving the future, it falls upon the ear like an 'old, old story,' and we heed it not. But we should heed it. For we are all servants and stewards, and must go soon to reckon with the Master.

"A little while" longer we may *give* to Him. Strange that the Owner and Ruler of all things, should want our gifts. But He does,—first our hearts, then our time, our talents, our property, our all. To speak of one of these, the silver and the gold, already his, He asks that it be laid at his feet and dedicated to the well-being of the race. Thousands there are who cheerfully respond to his claim; and among them, not a few upon whom He has lavished riches. It is better understood than it once was, that wealth has as well its responsibilities and duties as its privileges. An example like that of the great philanthropist* whose remains a Funeral-fleet such as the world scarcely ever saw before is now conveying to

---

* GEORGE PEABODY.

our shores, must continue to tell with power upon the Crœsuses and Midases of the world. While alone in the munificence of his benefactions, he is by no means alone in his generous concern for the welfare of his kind. There are instances of a kindred liberality in all our cities, and in many of our churches. We could all cite individuals who have made the noblest use of wealth, by devoting it to the bodily and the spiritual wants of the destitute. A happy facility for this is supplied by the number and variety of the objects which now invite sympathy and aid. If you shall ever, through the infinite mercy of God, stand among the ransomed above, you will not regret that you did something in this way for Him who, "though rich, for our sakes became poor, that we through his poverty, might be made rich." Remember his saying:—"Inasmuch as ye have done it unto one of the least of these my brethren, ye *have done it unto me.*" And do not forget the "little while."

We are none of us satisfied with our past *working*. Not to describe specific fields, there is Christian work needed on every side. And in every Church there are precious talents hidden in the earth, which the owners would do well to bring forth into use before the Master comes to look after his servants. Very cogent are the arguments which enforce this duty. Let it suffice that in "a little while" it will be too late. You would not like to see your Lord approaching just yet. You would fain help forward his cause in the world a little more. Up, then, for He will be here soon. Go work *to-day* in his vineyard—and *every* day. Thus would He choose to find you, and thus would you choose to meet Him. *This* obligation, also, is more widely felt than it once was.

It has happened here in our own Church, that when an individual was received into our communion, his very first question, before retiring from the presence of the Session, was,—"I wish to go to work: what have you for me to do?" And he went to work. The conviction is becoming general that a Christian profession implies *service*. It is not every one who can render it, in the form of philanthropic or missionary labor: infirm health, domestic ties, incessant toil, or other causes, may forbid. But active sympathy in the furtherance of the Gospel is the law of Christ's household; and it deeply behooves us to keep in mind the "little while."

No less helpful will this thought be to the *toilers* of the world. Everywhere the masses are shut up to a hard life—a life of incessant work with few comforts and many privations. Most benign is the promise of the Gospel to the poor who embrace its gracious offers. Your cup will lose its bitterness whenever you can realize that a Father's hand holds it to your lips. And the reflection—"a little while," will reconcile you to hardships, which, without some prospect of relief, might prove insupportable. By and by your appointed task will be finished, and you will go home to a long and peaceful rest, made twice welcome by the exhausting travail of the way.

And thus does the text proffer its grateful solace to the sick, the bereaved, the tempted, the impoverished, and all the tribes of want and sorrow. Let it inspire you with fresh patience and courage to reflect that in "a little while" your trials will be over—never to return.

Nor must I close without saying that while there is consolation here, there is admonition as well. To those who have 'neglected the great salvation,' there is a pregnant omen in the sound,—"a little while." Yes, it is, it *can* be, but a short time; yet eternal issues hang upon it. Can you afford to spend another year—which may, peradventure, prove only a few days or hours—without God and without hope?

Such, then, beloved, is the Scripture I come this morning to tender you, as your text for the New-Year. May it please God so to write it upon our hearts and imbue us with its spirit, that we may accept the labors and relaxations, the successes and reverses, the joys and sorrows, and all the changes of this year, with the abiding, cheerful, submissive, filial feeling—"A LITTLE WHILE."

XIII.

"THE LORD WILL GIVE GRACE AND GLORY."

PSALM LXXXIV. 11.

This is a text which cannot fail to satisfy you, expecting as you are this morning a motto for the year. Very urgent your cravings may be, very large your demands, and very lofty your aspirations, but they are all provided for here. When you utter the expression, 'grace and glory,' you condense into the briefest formula all that earth can need, and all that heaven can give.

Of course it is of his own the Most High speaks when He says, "The Lord will give glory." Promises like this pertain to the dowry of the saints; they are the jewelry of the Lamb's Bride, and no profane hands may appropriate them.

But some doubting Thomas may ask, "How am I to know this? What assurance have I that He will 'give grace and glory' to every one of his children?" The first reply is, because He has told them so. "Hath He said, and shall He not do it? Hath He spoken, and shall He not make it good?" The second is in the answer He made to the *first* Thomas, "Reach hither thy finger, and behold my hands; and reach hither thy hand, and thrust into my side; and be not faithless, but believing." What mean those wounds? Why did the Son of God become the Son of man, and die a malefactor's death? Was it to make a partial atonement for sin, to purchase for his people a precarious pardon, to afford them a taste of the Divine mercy, only to remit them to the inexorable custody of the law, with its retributive terrors? Rather is his crucifixion the pledge of all the blessings they can require in time or in eternity. "He that spared not his own Son, but delivered Him up for us all, how shall he not with him also freely give us all things?" To question this is to distrust a bond which is sealed with the blood of the Only Begotten.

The third answer is, that the immutable purpose of God has so bound these blessings together that one link of the chain necessarily draws all the other links after it. "Whom he did predestinate, them he also called: and whom he called, them he also justified: and whom he justified, them he also glorified." The effectual call of the believer implies his election, and involves his pardon, sanctification, and eternal glory.

Let these three grounds suffice to rebuke and cancel your misgivings. It is beyond controversy that "the Lord will give grace and glory," not to a few favored ones among his children, but to all alike, as well to the ignorant, the helpless, and the unknown, as to prophets, apostles, and martyrs. Here, again, is a crevice, through which unbelief creeps in. With your conscious ill desert you cannot imagine that He should regard *you* with the interest He bestows upon those of your fellow-men whose gifts greatly excel your own, and whose labors are more abundant. If you are not making a faithful use of your own advantages, this may be a good reason for humiliation. But to suppose that the mere possession of one talent or of five talents can affect the complacency with which God regards his children severally, and shut or open the gateways of his bounty towards them, is to mistake the organic law of the Mediatorial kingdom. Do not for an instant harbor the thought that He gives or denies us the blessings of the new covenant upon the basis of our personal endowments, or our personal merit or demerit. This were to import into the administration of his kingdom, a principle subversive of all grace, and most derogatory to the Redeemer. In fact what room were there, on this principle, for our text, and a thousand other precious Scriptures of like import? If grace and glory are the exclusive heritage of the *worthy*, where is the sinner or the saint who would presume to come forward and claim them? Small progress have we made even in the alphabet of our religion if we have yet to learn that "CHRIST is all and in all." To receive Christ is to receive all the benefits of his mediation. Not pardon only, nor renewal only, but all the graces and all the privileges of the new covenant are conveyed by that one imperial grant of the 'unspeakable gift.' He is 'made of God unto us wisdom and righteousness, sanctification, and redemption.' Believers are 'in Christ.' They are members of his body. When the Father looks upon them He sees them not as they are in themselves, but as they are in the Son of his love, and therefore alike *his* sons. Their life is hid in Christ's life—the source and means of their spiritual nourishment, the channel of all sacred influences to their souls.

This being the case, it becomes intelligible to us how the Sovereign Father can put all his people on the same footing, and can assure each one among them of 'grace and glory.' Not for *their* sakes is it done, not for any work or merit of their own; but for the sake of Him who died for their offences, and rose again for their justification. This detracts nothing from the love and mercy of their redemption. It leaves no room for self-complacency. It simply illustrates the infinite condescension and merit of the Saviour in expiating the sins and securing the ultimate triumph of a race so utterly without strength or goodness of their own.

We have hinted at the comprehensive nature of this promise, 'grace and glory.' Comprehensive it must needs be, or it would not suffice for us. "From me is thy fruit found." "Without me ye can do nothing." "In me (that is, in my flesh) dwelleth no good thing." "Not I, but the grace of God which was with me." There is no Christian whose heart will not respond a ready 'Amen' to utterances like these. And they show how indispensably we require Divine aid every day and hour of our lives.

We stand at the threshold of a new year, not knowing the things that are to befall us before its close. What we need just here is grace to commit ourselves into God's keeping without undue solicitude as to the future. Our text, then, comes into play at once. For nature is not wont to be tranquil in the presence (may I so speak?) of the future. It is to us what the dark is to children; we people it with untoward shapes and grim spectres. Or, rushing to the other extreme, like children anticipating the holidays, we replenish the future with visions of unmixed success and happiness. The lesson of Scripture is not that we frame no plans, take no precautions, indulge no hopes and expectations concerning the coming days and months, but that we do all this with a filial, confiding temper; that we reverently acknowledge God's universal providence; rely upon his wisdom and faithfulness, and trustfully leave all things with Him who is certain to do all things well. *This* is the duty of to-day; and for this our promise brings its unfailing grace.

While we cannot turn over a single leaf of the year's history (it requires a revolution of the globe on its axis to do that), we are certain of one thing. So long as life lasts, every day will bring to every one of us its round of familiar experiences. Great events are exceptional in the greatest lives. The world's captains, statesmen, inventors, authors, sages,—with these, no less than with the masses of mankind, life is made up substantially of littles. It is a routine of petty duties, petty trials, temptations, successes, interruptions, pleasures. If you keep a diary, how large a proportion of the pages, if candidly inscribed, would read: 'This day has passed like yesterday.' One photograph, slightly varied, would answer for perhaps five days out of six—that is for most people. Diversities there are; your school lessons are not quite identical through the week; you have some trouble with a child to-day which you did not have yesterday; your temper has given way rather more or rather less; you have had more or fewer visitors; you have had a fresh customer or two; you have had a cold or a headache, or got rid of one;—in some such tide as this life flows on with us day by day. When we consider man's origin and destiny, the immortality that awaits him, the possible indefinite expansion of his faculties, and his endless progression in knowledge, it does seem humiliating that he should spend the major part of the years allotted him here in such common-place employments. When I see a woman sitting for hours, with her needle in hand, taking one small stitch after another, and reflect that she is probably doing this day by day for months together, my first emotion is one of pity for the patient toiler, and the second a painful sense of the seeming incongruity there is between the ethereal, deathless nature, and an occupation like that. There is really no more reason for this feeling in the particular case specified than in many others of the usual domestic or mechanical occupations. The warp and woof of life is largely made up of a weaving which is simply a little more or a little less dignified than plying a needle for use or pastime. The stern rigor of our lot gives none of us respite from the clamorous demands for food, and drink, and repose. Wealth, and rank, and power, rather modify the shape and tone of these requisitions than annul them. We are *all* toilers, and the greater part of our toil is expended upon very common matters.

Now, what does this mean? And what use are we to make of it? Is it of chance that we are left to travel for so many years along these dead levels of life? Is there no significance but that which meets the eye in the stitching, and the washing, and the hammering, and the studying, and the nursing,—in the tame routine which marks off the dial between every sun-rising and sun-setting? Assuredly it *might* have been otherwise with us. With infinite resources at his command our Heavenly

Father could not have been shut up to precisely that type of economy under which we find ourselves. To concede this is to affirm that there were reasons, wise and good, which disposed Him to prefer this plan to any other; to some other, for example, which might have relieved at least his ransomed ones from a portion of their common tasks, and assigned them to pursuits more consonant (as *we* view things) to their exalted powers and destiny. If there be any mystery here this thought may help to resolve it.

God would prepare his children for heaven. This preparation includes of necessity not only forgiveness, but personal meetness. They must be moulded to a certain *character*. Having borne the image of the earthly, they must bear the image of the heavenly. They must be made holy, or they cannot dwell with a holy God. This points to a slow and tedious discipline. It is not a creation, but a growth. The leaven infused by the Divine Spirit must leaven the whole mass. The understanding, the affections, the will, the conscience, all require to be pervaded by it. Every faculty, every susceptibility, needs to be released from the bondage of sin, and brought into harmony with the word and will of God. Such a training requires time. It requires an indefinite variety of agencies and implements suited to each several part of the character. It demands—may we not say?—that the sort of atmosphere which surrounds the common walks of life be impregnated with a new vitality. For here, where we are off our guard, and there are no spectators to chide or cheer, the natural man finds his opportunity. The beaten paths of our daily toil reject the good seed, but give ready shelter and warmth to the tares. Selfishness, and discontent, and sloth, and irritability, and jealousy, and fretfulness, thrive here as in a hotbed. And what we need is strength to counteract these noxious tendencies. We must learn to regard these arid spaces as lying within the Lord's vineyard, and, it may be, as the very part He has given *us* to cultivate. The tillage may be very perplexing and exhausting, but what has that to do with duty? No friendly voices may encourage you in your toil, but be sure the Great Husbandman walks unseen along every one of those paths day by day, and, if faithful to your task, you shall not lack his commendation.

And just here it is our text comes to you with its timely promise. The Master well knew, in appointing you to this service, that you could not fulfil it without his aid. And so He pledges you his help. He will infallibly give you grace to honor Him in your common avocations. He can and will enable you to interweave with the texture of your current life the golden threads of patience, and content, and cheerfulness, and gratitude. He will make you to feel that the tamest service derives a certain dignity from the bare fact that He has laid it upon you. Flesh and blood might murmur if you could see nothing but the narrow walls and meagre furnishings of your room. But would you murmur if He should come to you every morning and say, with his gentle voice, 'Go, ply your needle to-day; go, drive the loom; go, wield the sledge; go, stand at the counter; go, teach the young; go, cast up figures; go, tread the dull routine of your domestic duties,—FOR ME?' So far from contemning your work, or halting under it, you would bless your Lord for the privilege of doing *anything* for Him. Your mouth would be filled with laughter, and your tongue with singing. The sterile paths under your feet would turn to 'living green.' And, far better still, your inner life would gather nourishment from these homely occupations, and gradually soar into a closer sympathy with the mind of Christ and the fellowship of the ransomed.

Let me, then, commend the text to you as a promise of needful help in the daily walks of life. Only seek his aid, and the Lord will give you grace which shall hallow your commonest occupations, and turn the laundry, the nursery, the refectory, the noisy workshop, the crowded mill, the blazing forge, the damp, dark mine, into a school where your higher nature shall triumph over sin and self, and acquire a growing meetness for the City of the Great King.

I have lingered upon this branch of my subject because, as familiar ground, it is of pre-eminent importance; and, again, because, in its relations to the pulpit, it is *not* 'familiar ground.' It is time now to glance in a passing way at some of the other treasures embosomed in our Scripture.

"The Lord will give grace and glory." We may carry the analysis of this word 'grace' very far without exhausting its meaning. It embraces, among other things, a promise of *Divine teaching and guidance*. Like all our former years, this year will bring us new proofs of our ignorance, and numerous questions which will baffle our sagacity. Difficulties are ever emerging out of the ordinary course of events which confound our skill and experience. Indeed, the wisest amongst us feel that they may find themselves at any hour of any day face to face with questions they know not how to deal with.

What a privilege to have an unfailing source to which we may repair for illumination! "I will instruct thee and teach thee in the way which thou shalt go: I will guide thee with mine eye." "The Lord God shall guide thee continually." "Thou shalt guide me with thy counsel, and afterward receive me to glory." This applies as well to the investigation of truth as to matters of practice. In this view we are in circumstances to appreciate its value. For, in the midst of the fervid evangelism of the day, while Bible societies are disseminating the Scriptures by the million, and missionary societies are sending Christian preachers into every land, two giant forms of error are rearing their heads at the opposite poles of Christendom. One is the hoary-headed Papacy, crowned and cursed with the blasphemous dogma of personal infallibility. The other is the pretentious and arrogant image of scientific Skepticism. At implacable enmity with each other, they wage a common war upon Jesus of Nazareth. One assumes to impose upon the consciences of men, by the sheer force of authority, the most profane lies as celestial truth. The other scornfully brands the most momentous truths, accredited by the authority of God Himself, as lies. Our young men are entering upon life at a period of general Pyrrhonism. The old foundations are to be torn up. Nothing is to be accepted as true upon evidence which has satisfied the ages. The most elementary theses, even to the immateriality of the soul, and the being of a God, are cast into the fiery alembic of philosophic unbelief, with the foregone conclusion that they are to be pronounced unworthy of credence. Superadd to this the controversies which subsist, as they always have subsisted, within the Church itself, and it will be seen how rare a blessing we have in the promise of Divine illumination. It is not a pretended but a real, infallible teacher, who has engaged to direct our inquiries. Alike to the young and the aged, to the wise and the simple, He proffers his gracious aid. There is no disciple perplexed with the inquiry, 'What is truth?' or embarrassed with the question, 'Whither does duty call me?' who is not warranted to ask and to expect the unerring counsel of the Great Teacher. For this is sealed to him in the promise, "The Lord will give grace and glory."

What is thus affirmed of enlightening and guiding grace is no less true of the grace we need *in the entire work of our sanctification.* We are called unto holiness. The end of the Christian life is conformity to God. To achieve this, is at once the most important and the most difficult service laid upon us. Of its difficulty we require no other proof than the imperfect sanctification of believers generally; rather let me say, no other proof than that supplied by our own experience. There is small occasion to go abroad and inspect the poor tillage of our neighbors' vineyards. Look at the weeds and thorns which deform our own. Not the same thorns and weeds in all; but, though diverse in species, they are one in nature. God has given you talents, and you have hidden them in the earth; the Church derives no benefit from them. He has bestowed property upon you, but you have not remembered the words of the Lord Jesus, how He said, It is more blessed to give than to receive. You are punctual in your attendance upon the sanctuary, but you are still more devoted to frivolous amusements. If you give your money freely for the spread of the Gospel, perhaps your Christianity fails to brighten your own home. You are zealous in mission and Sunday-school labors, but you are self-righteous and carping, unreasonable in your demands, and harsh in your judgments. These are simply specimen classes. If we are to credit what Christians say of one another, the Church is still the abode of legions of perverse tempers and evil habits. It is only here and there that a disciple appears who illustrates *all* the graces, and serves to show by contrast how far we, most of us, fall short of what we profess and ought to be.

This state of things, at once so humiliating and so instructive, exhibits in the strongest light the greatness of our work, and the hopelessness of accomplishing it by any resources of our own. Instead of marvelling at the errors and defects so common among Christians, a thoughtful observer may deem it matter of surprise and gratitude that religion should survive at all from age to age. There is ample room for this emotion, if we exclude the idea of a constant Divine interposition. Let me explain.

A few days since I received from a kind friend a quarto volume, entitled *Flowers from the Upper Alps, with Glimpses of their Homes.* Very beautiful it is as a work of art, and very true to nature. I turned over the leaves and looked, one after another, at these delicate plants, sending up their slender shafts, and unfolding their many tinted petals to the sunbeam, or spreading their rich tapestry of vines over the barren rock, some with a mere hand-breadth of soil, laid bare by an avalanche, into which to strike their roots, and all of them shut in by everlasting snows. And it did seem wonderful that flowers could bud and bloom up there among the perpetual glaciers, eight and nine thousand feet above the sea. While I was admiring the infinite wisdom and might of Him who had endowed them with the subtle alchemy which can extract nutriment from the frost-laden winds of that region, it occurred to me that these flowers are apt symbols of *the Christian in the world.* His home is among barren rocks and ice-fields. The atmosphere he breathes is surcharged with deadly poisons. The whole structure and tendencies of things around him are destructive to his better principles. All the currents of earthly influence he encounters bear him away from God and heaven. And yet he is *not* overwhelmed. His life does not go out. In many instances it grows up into strength and vigor. It thrives upon the elements organized for its extinction. With a chemistry not surpassed by that of the Alpine flora, it extracts nourishment from an air laden with miasma, and transmutes the very storms that sweep over it into means and appliances of healthful growth. Of both phenomena we may say, "'This also cometh forth from the Lord of Hosts, which is wonderful in counsel and excellent in working." No other solution is admissible. We may exclaim of any one who has lived a pious and useful life, 'What hath God wrought!' For it is *all* of God.

Here lies our whole encouragement,—that He should consent to keep this work in his own hands, and do for us what we could never do for ourselves. The urgency of the work is beyond dispute. There is nothing of higher moment to us than that we grow in grace. If the past year has come and gone without seeing us advanced in holiness, with the old tempers and habits as robust, and the new life as feeble as ever, then sin lieth at our door. And this sin will gather fresh power and turpitude if we take it with us, unrepented of, into the engagements of the new year. Let it be deeply impressed upon our minds to-day that, whatever else be neglected, the soul's wants *must* be cared for; that it will not do to trust to a superficial, a one-sided, or a periodical, religion; that there is a glaring deficiency in any style of piety which illumines the head, but does not permeate the heart; that excites the imagination, but does not subjugate the will; that influences the passions, but does not inform and arouse the conscience; that makes its possessor punctilious in his observance of sacraments, but leaves him a devotee of the world; that sends him out an earnest worker in the broad field of philanthropy, but holds him a miserable bond-slave to unlovely tempers. All these are incongruities which need to be guarded against. We constantly admonish the unconverted that they simply mock God and deceive themselves by supposing that He will consent to strike the balance between their good deeds and their bad ones, and so render the award of life or death. As little warrant is there for a Christian professor to offset one part of his Christianity, in which he imagines himself to excel, against another part in which he is grossly deficient. It is the *entire* man which the Master claims, the unreserved surrender of *all* the powers and members, the loving obedience of the heart to every one of his precepts, the gradual assimilation of the whole character and life to his own image.

To this work God's word and the Holy Spirit are ever inviting us. And the opening year clothes the invitation with peculiar solemnity and tenderness. Futile it were to go about it in our own strength; but He does not ask this, nor would He smile on it. 'He will give grace and glory.' If we have not been dealing in exaggerated phrases, it is no common measure of grace we shall require to carry us over the obstructions of the way. But great and small belong to *our* vocabulary. They are nothing to God. With Him all things are possible. What He offers to you now, He has bestowed upon ten thousands of his people. He has over and over renewed the miracle of the Alpine flowers before your eyes, in so strengthening, sustaining, and maturing some disciple you have known and loved that his character has been radiant with spiritual beauty, and his life has been a benediction to many. The same grace is tendered to you, as ample in measure and as *free*, in answer to prayer. Prove Him now, if it be not so. Dedicate this year to Him. Be no longer content with your crude attainments. Resolve upon a deeper sounding into the depths of the Divine promises, a more thorough divorce from the world, a more faithful culture of *all* the graces of the Spirit, a more consistent, holy, and fruitful life. This is within the reach of every Christian here. It will be our loss and sin if we come short of it, for He will not fail in his part. 'He *will* give grace and glory.'

Grace for still other uses we shall need in the course of this year. If for nothing else, certainly for *trials and sorrows*. No year has yet passed over us without leaving in some households here a record chronicled in tears. It were a fond conceit to suppose that the coming twelvemonth is to be in this respect unlike all that have preceded it. In what guise trouble is to come, upon whom it is to fall, how soon, and with what concomitants,—all these points are happily concealed from us. What more deeply concerns us, is, that for every form of trouble the Divine word brings its consolation. No storm ever yet beat upon a Christian's head for which there was not some support or shelter provided in the immutable covenant. The grace assured to God's children enables them to realize that their losses and perplexities, their sicknesses and bereavements, are appointed by a Father's love. This confidence changes the whole aspect of the dispensation. It recruits their faith and hope. It brings them to the mercy-seat. It unseals to them the promises. It blunts the power of sense. It detaches the affections from earth, and leads them upward to God. It replaces human loves in the breast with love to the Saviour. It not only inculcates, but inspires, resignation. It sustains the stricken believer in passing through the waters and the fire. It takes away the sting of death, and dries the mourner's tears. All this, and more than this, the grace of God can do for his children,—the grace which is pledged to you in the precious text before us. Amidst the uncertainties of the year now dawning, it is an unspeakable comfort to know that no trial can come without his permission, and none for which He has not already provided either full deliverance or an adequate support.

This pertains no less to public than personal calamities. The signs of the times seem to prelude a year of momentous changes, of mighty convulsions, that are to shake continents to their centre, and deluge them with blood. There is much in the condition of Christendom to try the faith of intelligent and devout believers, and

the prospect is that their faith will be cast into a still more fiery crucible before the year closes. But, for these troubles, as well as for their private afflictions, the promise brings plenary strength, and patience, and comfort :—
"The Lord will give grace and glory."

> "Let mountains from their seats be hurled
> Down to the deep, and buried there,
> Convulsions shake the solid world,
> Our faith shall never yield to fear."

"Grace and *glory!*" The treasures bound up in the first of these words have engrossed our thoughts. We have taken only a step or two in exploring the riches garnered up in this word, which is itself a mere vestibule to the other. The two are indissolubly united. The grant which makes over *grace* to the believer carries *glory* in its bosom also. The pledge of present grace is the earnest of future glory, and this not by arbitrary decree but because glory is as essentially enfolded in grace as the flower is in the seed, and the oak in the acorn.

How this expands our year-text! How it enlarges your heritage! How it floods those common walks of life of which we were speaking with the splendors of the empyrean! How it dignifies every service that bears the sacred name of duty! How it dwarfs the trials of life, and solaces its griefs, and turns its lamentations into hosannas! All that it means, nor man, nor angel knows. What we *do* know of it, I shall not attempt to set forth. Enough that your charter includes whatever of purity and peace, of dignity and honor, of perfect rest and everlasting felicity, may be intended by that fathomless word, 'glory.' Ponder it, Christian brethren, on this New Year's morning. Take it into your heart of hearts; cherish it as a sacred talisman wherever you go; keep it in mind as you launch forth upon this untraversed sea, that whatever its shoals and reefs, its storms and wrecks, 'grace and glory' await you. In every emergency, in the presence of temptation, under the burden of your daily toil, on a bed of sickness, when smitten with a great sorrow, when training for some arduous service, in combating corruption within or iniquity without, in your prosperous ease, in your hours of despondency, recall the priceless promise, "The Lord will give grace and glory." Peradventure, you may need its help—some of us inevitably will—in a yet more solemn conjuncture. There are many vacant seats at your boards, and in these pews, which were filled on the last New Year's Sabbath. The Scripture then proposed to you, "*A little while,*" proved a prophetic utterance to not a few whom we tenderly loved, and would fain have kept with us. Can we doubt that this experience will repeat itself during the present year? Our loved ones, departed in the faith and hope of the Gospel, now comprehend, as it is not possible for us to do, the deep, hidden meaning of our New Year text, 'grace and glory.' They know more of 'grace' than the most mature believer who is still in the flesh; first, because they have received not only living grace but dying grace; and, secondly, because the boundless grace of redemption can never be appreciated until the august scheme is contemplated from heaven. And, then, we know *nothing* of 'glory;' whereas they are robed with all its splendors, and filled with all its blessedness. This is alike for the encouragement of the pilgrims whose feet may be soon pressing the margin of Jordan, and for the comfort of those whose friends have crossed the stream.

Of some who have within the last few months passed from grace into glory I would gladly speak, would time and strength permit. But I must content myself with the expression of a pastor's sincerest sympathy with your afflictions, and with the hope and prayer that to you, and to *all* my people, there may come the utmost fulness of blessing which can be bound up in our grateful benediction, A HAPPY NEW YEAR!

In thus passing by our own sorrows, I shall have your indulgence for a word respecting that recent dispensation which has cast its shadows upon *all* our churches, upon our whole land, almost upon the Christian world. "There is a prince and a great man fallen in Israel!" Our city has paused in the midst of the festivities of the season to gather around his bier. Eloquent eulogy, more just than eulogy is wont to be, has commemorated his rare gifts, and still rarer graces. Devout men have carried him to his burial, and made great lamentation over him; and the tears of two generations bedew his grave. I will not repeat, though I heartily endorse, the emphatic tributes paid to his various learning, his intellectual power, his prodigious industry, his quiet, unassuming carriage, his consistent example, and his laborious, beneficent, and useful life. These and their kindred traits have been fitly lauded. But I cannot forbear expressing the sense of personal bereavement I feel in the death of Mr. BARNES. While differing widely in some of our theological views, this was no bar to our friendship. I gave him my cordial esteem, my veneration, my love. And he left me no room to doubt that he reciprocated the affection I bore him. It was always a pleasure to me to meet him. Whenever we were thrown together, we were sure to have refreshing converse upon topics of private interest or public importance; and there were grave questions touching the economics of the Church, upon which our sentiments coalesced, in opposition to opinions current among younger men of *all* 'schools.' In parting with him on these occasions, it was uniformly with a deepened impression of his sincerity, his purity, his conscientiousness, and his supreme devotion to the work God had given him to do. A presence like his was a perpetual benediction to his brethren. The withdrawal of it creates a void in the ranks of the Christian ministry of our city which no survivor can fill. Let us bless God for the 'grace' which shone so conspicuously in his character and life, and for the 'glory' into which he was so suddenly translated. Help us, O Lord, to 'follow them who, through faith and patience, have inherited the promises;' and 'make us to be numbered with thy saints in glory everlasting!'

XIV.

"WHOSE I AM, AND WHOM I SERVE."

ACTS xxvii. 23.

VERY remarkable language this is, whether we consider the person who uttered it, or the circumstances in which he was placed at the time. You will readily recall that memorable voyage of the great Apostle of the Gentiles, on his way as a prisoner to Rome, when the frail bark, with its large freight of human beings, encountered a hurricane of two weeks' duration, and the whole company were expecting certain death. In the midst of this turmoil, while the winds and waves were hurrying them on, as they believed, to inevitable destruction, for "all hope (so we read) that we should be saved was then taken away,"—at this critical conjuncture, Paul stood forth before the "two hundred threescore and sixteen souls," his fellow-voyagers, and addressed to them these calm, assuring words:—"Sirs, ye should have hearkened unto me, and not have loosed from Crete, and to have gained this harm and loss. And now I exhort you to be of good cheer: for there shall be no loss of any man's life among you, but of the ship. For there stood by me this night the angel of God, *whose I am, and whom I serve,* saying, Fear not, Paul; thou must be brought before Cæsar: and lo, God hath given thee all them that sail with thee. Wherefore, sirs, be of good cheer: for I believe God, that it shall be even as it were told me. Howbeit we must be cast upon a certain island." Brave words these in the face of such a tornado! And how literally they were verified by the result, you well know. Many topics they suggest upon which we cannot now dwell. Let it simply be noted, in passing, that this whole ship's company were saved for the sake of one Christian man. " So God hath *given thee* all them that sail with thee." If the irreligious knew how many blessings, temporal no less than spiritual, come to them purely for the sake of Christian relatives or friends, it might do something to conciliate their kindly regards towards that Gospel they contemn. Possibly there may be those *here* whose life has been prolonged for another year, chiefly for the sake of some pious wife, or parent, or child, with whose faith they have not the slightest sympathy.

I have spoken of the text as a remarkable utterance;—remarkable, very, if we assume a latent reference to the Lord Jesus Christ. This we seem warranted in doing, because Paul repeatedly styles himself "a servant of Jesus Christ," and is followed herein by his fellow-Apostles, Peter and Jude. Reverting to his early history, it reveals the thorough transformation which had passed over him that he should use language of this sort. There was a period when hatred of Jesus Christ was the controlling passion of his nature,—a hatred all the more intense and malevolent because nursed as a religious sentiment, and sanctified by the vigils and prayers of the strictest of devotees. Now, not merely is his hatred turned to love, but he exults in bearing to that same Jesus the relation of a bondman. In the passage before us—'whom I serve,' the precise meaning of the verb is to *serve* in the way of *worship*, the highest form of service, and involving every other type. But elsewhere he uses the word δουλος. He even puts it, in his opening salutation to the Roman Church, as the most honorable of titles, and meet to be associated with the high office of Apostleship:—" Paul, a δουλος, a *bondman*, a *slave* of Jesus Christ, called to be an Apostle, ... to all that be in Rome." In this view, the two phrases in the text, "Whose I am, and whom I serve," are explanatory of each other. "I belong to Christ; his ownership in me is as complete as that of a Roman master in his slave." Nothing could go beyond this. And his whole life attested how truly he felt it, and how heartily he gloried in it.

While there were many things in St. Paul's character and history peculiar to himself, there was very much in his experience that he shared with the faithful of all lands and generations. Every true disciple sustains the same relation to Jesus Christ that he did. Every one *professes* what Paul avows here,—"Whose I am, and whom I serve." We have all appropriated this language, my brethren. We virtually make it our own, not only so often as we sit down at the Lord's table, but in every prayer we offer, and every psalm of praise we sing. It cannot be amiss, then, to inquire what these words mean, and how far it may be helpful to carry them with us into the scenes of the opening year.

"Whose I am." Here is an acknowledgment on the

part of the believer of God's absolute property or ownership in him. *Whence does it originate?*

Manifestly, believers belong to God by the right of *creation*. He who made us, owns us. No right can be more unqualified or indefeasible than this. But as it applies to all men not only, but to all creatures, animate and inanimate, material and spiritual, it would not be pertinent to press it in this connection.

In the second place, believers belong to Christ, because *they were given Him by the Father in the covenant of grace.*

In no obscure terms do the Scriptures instruct us of this sublime transaction between the Father and the Son. Foreseeing the apostacy of our first parents, and the consequent ruin of their posterity, it pleased God from eternity to ordain that certain of our race should be restored to his favor and image. Those whom He thus set his love upon He gave to his only begotten Son, who, on his part, engaged to become their surety and ransom. "According as he hath chosen us in him (Christ) before the foundation of the world." "Who hath saved us and called us with an holy calling, not according to our works, but according to his own purpose and grace, which was given us in Christ Jesus before the world began." "I pray not for the world, but for them which thou hast given me; for they are thine." In terms like these does the inspired word refer to the sovereign and gracious purpose of God in determining to rescue a portion of mankind from the sway of his and their great enemy. As all were alike guilty, miserable, and helpless, so, left to themselves, all must have remained in that state perpetually. His right to bestow certain of them—all, had

He so chosen—upon the Son of his love, was perfect. The right of the Son to accept the gift upon the conditions of the covenant of grace, was no less perfect. And by the same token is his ownership in all true Christians established upon an immutable foundation.

Another of the pillars upon which this claim rests is *redemption*. Of this august theme, which lights up the sacred records from Genesis to Revelation, it must suffice to say, that the Son of God fulfilled to the letter the stipulations of that covenant of which we have just spoken. Very affecting it is to reflect how much was to be done—aye, and how much to be suffered—before a single sinner of our race could be brought into a situation in which he might lift his eyes heavenward and say, "Whose I am!" Infinite love was on the throne, and infinite wisdom, and infinite power. But, without an expiation, not all the infinites combined could avail to roll back the curse which had overwhelmed man. Bethlehem was a stern necessity; Gethsemane was a necessity; Calvary was a necessity. The Only-begotten, dwelling in the glory which He had with the Father before the world was, knew it all; yet did He freely offer himself as our ransom; and, when the fulness of the time was come, He as freely assumed our nature, and bore our sins in his own body on the tree. Thus was the eternal compact crowned and sealed with his own blood. "Christ hath redeemed us from the curse of the law, being made a curse for us." Henceforth his people are doubly his; his by the Father's gift, and his by the efficacy of his atoning death. The spotless righteousness thus wrought out by Him as their substitute is made theirs. There *can*, therefore, be 'no condemnation' to them, for they are 'in Christ Jesus.' Liberated from the old bondage, and engrafted into Christ, they belong to Him as really as the branch belongs to the vine. Well may they say, "Whose I am," for their very life, their *whole* life, is derived from Him!

Yet it is not derived from Christ without the intervention of an agent, who shares with Him the work of man's recovery. The believer belongs to Christ by reason of the radical change wrought in his character by the Divine Spirit. What we are by nature, was symbolized by that valley of dry bones seen in vision by the prophet. What the redeemed become by grace, is shown by that white-robed company around the throne. The moral distance lying between these extremes is something immense. Never could it have been traversed, never could the first step of the way have been taken by a single sinner of Adam's race, but for the mission of the Holy Spirit to our world. Even the cross of Christ—that spectacle which concentrates upon itself the rapt gaze of all the angelic hosts—must have been set up in vain. Men would have passed and re-passed it, age after age, with as little of relenting or sympathy as was exhibited by the callous throng who poured that day out of the gates of Jerusalem to witness the crucifixion. The blessed Spirit came to rescue man from himself, to open his eyes, to unseal his ears, to subjugate his will, and to lead him a willing, grateful penitent, to the Saviour. Not reluctantly now, but joyfully, does he bend his neck to receive the yoke of Christ. And henceforth it becomes the guiding maxim of his life,—"Whose I am."

This is anticipating the only remaining consideration I shall adduce to show the absolute ownership which

Christ has in his people, viz., their voluntary choice of Him as their Master, and their covenant engagement to know no other Lord.

I say, their *voluntary* choice, for no act of their lives can be more so. Through the secret, silent, and irresistible influence of the Spirit of God, their enmity is turned to love. Up to this period they could not hear the voice of Christ; now all the tumult of earth cannot drown it. They would not come to Him that they might have life; now they cannot stay away from Him. It is in their eyes a proof of his boundless love and pity that He should be willing to receive them, that He should consent to give them a place among those happy 'bondmen' of his, whose bondage is perfect freedom. And, approaching Him in this temper, their grateful song goes up before Him :—

> "Thy grace so costly, yet so free,
> My hope and song shall ever be,
> Till, in thy courts above,
> In loftier, sweeter notes I'll sing
> The praises of my Saviour King,
> And his redeeming love."

Such is our answer to the question, 'What are the elements which constitute this intimate relationship between Christ and the believer, in virtue of which every Christian can say, and does say, "Whose I am ?" There is, first, the eternal decree of the Father; next, the ransom paid by the Son; then, the renewing work of the Divine Spirit; and, to crown all, the hearty, thankful consent of the believing sinner. Here is a fourfold bond— a bond so strong that nothing in earth, or heaven, or hell, can ever sunder it. It makes the ownership of Christ in his people so absolute that nothing could make it more so. They are his body and soul. Whatever they own He owns. Their property is his. Their gifts and accomplishments are his. He owns their homes and their business. He owns their health, their time, their influence, and their all. He so owns them and theirs that He can dispose of them as He may choose. Subject only to the restrictions imposed by his own rectitude, He may assign them to any sphere, appoint them to any service, visit them with any trials, exact of them any sacrifice, He sees fit. His own most holy will is the only rule by which He is bound in his dealings with them. And they would not have it otherwise. It was with this clear understanding they consented to the compact. And their ready response to his every demand is, "Whose I am, and whom I serve."

What this service involves, is implied in the remarks already made. But we must consider the question more minutely if we are to carry the text with us into the scenes of the coming year. Three things it comprehends, to wit:—

Faith in all Christ's teachings.
Obedience to all his commands.
And submission to all his allotments.

1. *Faith in all Christ's teachings.* It pertains to the relation in which we stand to Christ, that we recognize Him as our prime instructor, and accept his lessons with an implicit faith. This imports a careful study of his word, that we may learn what He has caused to be written for our benefit. That the word should contain 'some things hard to be understood,' is a matter of course.

When we consider that the sacred books were penned by numerous authors, dispersed over a period of sixteen centuries; that they treat of a vast variety of topics pertaining to different countries and peoples; and, especially, that they discourse of the loftiest themes upon which the minds of men or angels could be employed, it were a greater marvel than any they now present to us, if they had not embraced " things hard to be understood."

Nor is it strange that thoughtful and conscientious readers should sometimes hesitate and doubt over these recondite revelations. This need not impeach their fidelity to the Master, provided they have an honest desire to learn what He teaches, and are using the proper means to that end. To reject a doctrine simply because it is 'too high' for their narrow comprehension, or because it does not seem to them to be 'reasonable,' would be quite incompatible with the allegiance they owe Him. If it be out of 'a true heart' you say, "Whose I am, and whom I serve," you will search the Scriptures as for hid treasures; you will seek, by earnest study and prayer, to have your doubts and difficulties, on whatever points, removed; you will labor for a deeper insight into the 'great mystery of godliness' and its related topics; you will cordially accept the truth as it may be made plain to you; and you will be satisfied only with an *intelligent* Christianity, which adds to its faith and virtue an ever-increasing *knowledge* of the inspired word.

2. The service of Christ includes *obedience to all his commands.*

It were superfluous to argue the question whether a servant owes fealty to his master. Here is the best of all Masters, and here are the most favored of all servants—

bondmen, who have a nobler distinction in being called to serve such a Master, than they would have had in ruling over an earthly kingdom. The service they have pledged to Him is unconditional, without "ifs" or "buts." It is universal, extending to *all* requirements. It is constant, terminating only with life. It is sincere, emanating from a loving heart, and animated by a cheerful spirit.

3. No less vital, as one of the elements of this service, is *submission to all Christ's allotments*.

There is a familiar type of submission, the deference which is paid to authority, the homage which power exacts of dependence. Essentially servile in its nature, it is the poles away from the sentiment here intended. Genuine submission springs from love. It does not exclude sensibility to trials. So far from it, a gracious person—one who has experienced the renewing of the Holy Ghost—has all his sensibilities quickened, and his affections refined to that degree that he feels more keenly than ever before. But he believes in a Providence. He has confidence in the wisdom and faithfulness of his Heavenly Father. He sees God's hand as well in his trials as in his mercies. And, however painful they may be to flesh and blood, he supplicates the grace which may enable him to say, "Thy will be done!" *This* is Christian resignation.

Other particulars proper to the exposition of the text will readily suggest themselves to your minds; but enough has been said to prepare the way for that application of the subject which the occasion demands.

There lies before you, we will suppose, your "*Diary for* 1872;" all but its first six pages as yet untouched by the pen. You are now asked to write at the top of each one of these spotless pages the inscription, "Whose I am, and whom I serve." What does this import? Clearly that you are to carry into every day the conviction that you are not your own, but Christ's; that He has bought you with a price no less than his own blood; and that you are to serve Him with all your powers of body and mind, of heart and soul. His right to this service will be contested. Other masters will claim your homage. His rule is one which does not suit the world; and the world, therefore, frames statutes of its own. These conventional codes vary indefinitely in different ages and countries, but they are all more or less incompatible with his law. They sanction practices which He would frown upon. They confuse the elements of right and wrong; and, for the immutable principles of truth and duty, substitute maxims of expediency, which have neither uniformity nor legitimate authority. No man who feels that he may lawfully do whatever his neighbors do, can appropriate the language of the text, except through a perverted conscience. The pressure from this quarter to be resisted is sometimes very great. One does not like to be singular. It is not pleasant to forego, for example, in buying and selling, usages which one's rivals are employing to the enlargement of their profits. It is quite natural to fall in with the tone and temper of the community or fraternity to which we belong. Many an upright man has come by degrees to countenance the flagitious gambling which is the opprobrium of some stock exchanges. Americans are apt to be revolted when they first witness the systematic desecration of the Sabbath in foreign capitals; but a brief residence often proves sufficient to draw them into the noxious current. We take on unconsciously the hues reflected from our daily associations, and are content with being no worse than our fellows. These, we persuade ourselves, are better than an 'over-scrupulous' moralist might concede; but their real position is too often that defined by the disciple whom Jesus loved:—"They are of the world; therefore speak they of the world, and the world heareth them." Yet it is to such hands the sceptre is quietly transferred by those who had no *conscious* purpose of wresting it from the hands that bear the print of the nails.

Allegiance to Christ cannot consort with this subserviency to a world which nailed Him to the tree. "No man can serve two masters." We profess to have decided between them. If it be in good faith that we have inscribed our daily journal with the motto, "Whom I serve," we must listen to his voice only, not to the clamorous voices of the world, and not even to the voice of the Church, unless we be entirely sure that Christ is speaking *through* the Church. For is it not too apparent that the counsels of the Church, if not as an organized society, at least of many who use its dialect, and share its privileges, are at variance with *his* counsels? Every one has seen how the Church and the world have been gravitating towards each other of late years,—whether by a growing deflection of both orbits, or of only one of them, people will decide for themselves. That the *tendency* of the Church is earthward, that it was so even when Apostles were its teachers, is apparent, not simply from the New Testament, and from ecclesiastical history, but from the personal experience of believers. For the society must represent the individuals that compose it; and every Christian is painfully aware of the energy with which he is ever drawn towards the things that perish with the using! Were it not that these tendencies are counteracted or modified by gracious influences from without, what Christian, what Church, could escape final shipwreck?

With what reason, then, can any believer assume as his rule of duty the opinions or customs of his brethren, unless he have first verified them by the Master's utterances? How far your associates are worthy to be implicitly imitated you may learn with sufficient accuracy by interrogating your own heart. They are, probably, very much what you are, not essentially better nor worse. If it be right for you to take them as your model, they must have the same warrant to take you for theirs. Are you ready for this? Do you feel that it would be wise on their part? Is it the dictate of conscience that your brethren would do well to tread in your steps, especially in relation to that large class of mixed questions concerning which consciences may differ? An Apostle could say, "Brethren, *be followers together of me*, and mark them which walk, so as ye have us for an example." But who amongst *us* would venture to address his brethren in this strain? "One is your Master, even Christ." *Here* is the lesson we profess to have learned. And it is clothed with the highest possible significance, because it is Christ Himself who speaks. If we honestly accept this truth, we cannot put upon Him the indignity of consulting our fellow-servants in preference to the Master. Let them say or do what they please, right or wrong, wise or foolish. They are no law to us. "Be not ye the servants of men." They cannot answer for us, nor we for them.

Enough that we have our Master, and are responsible to Him alone.

Should it happen, then, in the course of this year, that you are solicited to take this or that debatable step mainly upon the ground that it has the sanction of some "good Christians," it will be well to recall our year-text and say to yourself, "Whose I am, and whom I serve! What will my MASTER have me do?" Happily, you can consult Him. It is one of our great advantages that He is always at hand. No emergency of this sort can arise that we may not lay the question before Him, with a reasonable assurance that He will guide us to the proper conclusion. With his word in our hands, and the Spirit's aid freely promised, the path will ordinarily be made so plain that "wayfaring men, though fools, need not err therein." Shall we not begin the year with the habit of consulting the Master on all questions of duty?

It is no unusual custom, in well-ordered families, for servants to come to the head of the household each morning and receive instructions for the day. Doubtless this is your own habit in respect to *your* Master. But, peradventure, it may sometimes be slighted, or the instructions may be soon forgotten. Suppose you go to Him reverently and trustfully, and ask his directions for the new year. 'Thine I am, O Lord, and Thee I serve. What hast Thou for me to do this year? How can I turn my gifts and opportunities to the best account? Wherein can I serve Thee most acceptably?'

A petition like this, followed up by correspondent *daily* petitions, would, in the course of a twelvemonth, save us a world of perplexity, and simplify the work of life as much as it would augment our comfort. It is not improbable that the Master might answer our inquiries in part by reminding us wherein we had failed of our duty in past years. The era of direct revelation has gone by. But He still speaks to us 'in divers manners;' and one of the books He puts in our hands is our own biography. Very diverse are the uses to be made of it; but no one of them is of higher moment than the admonitions it supplies of our mistakes and sins, and the necessity of avoiding them in the future. What they may have been we cannot specify for one another. Each life makes its own record. A faithful memory, aided by a quickened conscience, will preach to you of the past as no other preacher can. It will be your wisdom to heed its counsels, even though they come to you in the form of reproaches for wasted time and neglected duties.

In regard to the particular sphere we are to occupy, there are not many amongst us to whom that is an open question. Providence has assigned us to our positions, and prescribed our vocations. But it remains to be decided in what spirit we are to meet the obligations of our allotted task. You will have gone sometimes into a mill where a hundred men were engaged at the same mechanical processes, and you must have observed not only their different grades as to aptitude and skill, but the diversity they exhibited in respect of the diligence and alacrity with which they plied their work. It is not enough that we go through our allotted task, and so complete the day's service, whether in the factory or the shop, the sick-room or the forum, the library or the legislative hall, that no human tongue may have cause to upbraid us. The eye of the '*Great* Taskmaster' is upon us, and if our eye be upon Him also, it will put us upon carry ing into our work the utmost energy we can command, and a serenity of temper that shall prove how *willing* a service we are paying Him. It is a Divine act, that of prosecuting our ordinary pursuits with an habitual and grateful reference to his will. Those who have learned the lesson will attest that there is nothing which aids so effectually in smoothing the rough paths of toil and lightening its burdens as the feeling that all these arrangements are of God's appointment, and that the myriad tribes of labor are *his* servants.

Nor are these the limits of the Almighty domain. It covers no less our civil relations. The state is one of his institutions. Your political obligations terminate upon Him, and these are to be as conscientiously discharged as are your religious duties. Were this principle adequately recognized by Christian men generally, it would produce a revolution in the country more decisive and more benign than any which has ever crowned the triumph of a political party. What a reproach it is to the Christianity of the land that it shrinks so much from contact with the *politics* of the land, as though in giving us what we boast of as "the best government in the world," it were a matter of indifference to the Great Supreme whether we took care of it, or suffered it to degenerate into anarchy or despotism. What sort of fealty is that which is rendered to Christ when his servants by the thousand stand idly by and see vile men nominated and elected to important offices without resisting it? The country looks aghast at the frightful official corruption which has been unearthed of late. It might have been prevented. To a large extent it would have been prevented if the *religious men* of all parties had been true to the motto inscribed upon that ensign which they *profess* to carry high above their party banners, "Whose I am, and whom I serve." No, no, brethren, you have *not* been true to your profession. All over the land Christian men have often gathered around party standards held by the foulest hands, while the blood-stained *Labarum* of their glorious leader has been trailed in the dust. It will be one step towards the redressing of the wrongs which *you* may have had some agency in visiting not only upon the commonwealth but upon the cause of Christ, if you henceforth discard the pestilent heresy that the politics of the country are a worthless common, where the scum of the populace are to hold their revels and plan their robberies, instead of a garden to be cultivated by the choicest hands, and seeded with the finest of the wheat. The country needs your help, and has a right to demand it. If the offices it claims are distasteful to you, remember who it is that has laid them upon you, and consider what must have been your condition to-day if Christ had declined all offices that were not agreeable to his natural feelings. To attempt to divorce your religion from the claims of citizenship is not merely disloyalty to your country, it is perfidy to Christ.

We pass, by a grateful transition, from the State to the Church. Here the inscription is too legible to be hid, and we meet it on every side,—"Whose I am, and whom I serve!" And, again, the inquiry recurs, How am I to carry this sentiment with me into the experiences of the year? Manifestly (for one thing) by leaving at its threshold whatever might impede you in your work. When you visit a neighbor through rain and mud, you put off your soiled coverings as you enter his house; good breeding and your own comfort require it. We have all been on the move for twelve months, with varying skies, with ever-shifting scenes, with companions, friendly, hostile, or indifferent, of every tone and temper, and it will not be strange if we have brought accretions with us which should be dropped before we go any further. There are, possibly, some untoward habits that have been contracted, some vicious appetites indulged, some prejudices nursed, some rude antipathies paraded, some selfish aspirations fostered. Would it not be well, now that the new year is throwing open its door to us, to leave these outside? They will only be a clog to us, and an annoyance to others, if we insist upon keeping them. Better to let them drift away upon the broad bosom of the old year, which is fast bearing so many *better* things out of sight. We shall have thorny places to traverse, and burdens to take up, and perils to encounter, and battles to wage, before *this* year is over; and it behooves us to get rid of all possible incumbrances at the start, to 'lay aside every weight, and the sin which doth so easily beset us, that we may run with patience the race set before us,' and 'fight the good fight of faith, and lay hold upon eternal life.'

This is *preparation* for work. For the work itself, so there be a willing mind, the Master will show us where and how we may serve Him to good purpose. His vineyard is very large. There is room for all that care to labor, and there is work for all. Our part of the field may not be just that which we should prefer. Our functions may be less conspicuous than those of some others. The probable results may be comparatively moderate. To turn a lathe all day, to drive the shuttle, to delve in a mine, to ply the needle, to plod through the monotonous routine of housewifery day by day, with the bare necessaries of life to keep the domestic machinery in motion,—all this must be trying enough to flesh and blood. What wonder if the servants employed in these vocations look sometimes with a wistful—I will not say an envious—eye, towards others, their fellow-servants, who are assigned to a richer soil, with better implements, an easier tillage, and, prospectively, a more generous harvest? If you pause with the outward and the sensible here, repining is inevitable. But, if you recall your lesson, "Whose I am, and whom I serve," you will not repine. He distributes his gifts to his servants, and sends them to their work, as He deems best. What He expects of them is, not that they display equal abilities, or master the same acquisitions, or attract the same attention, or achieve the same results. Nothing of this. But that they be faithful each to *his own* trust. The remark of John Newton has been often quoted, that if God should send two angels into the world, and order one to drive a team, and the other to rule a kingdom, they would be equally satisfied with their respective positions. To be "a servant of the Lord Jesus Christ" is distinction enough for man or angel; the *day* will so declare it. The proper antidote to despondency on the part of the toiling disciple, and to pride on the part of his affluent, or eloquent, or eminently useful, brother, lies in the reflection, "Whose I am, and whom I serve."

It were easy to adduce scores of arguments by way of commending this Scripture to you as your guide and talisman for the year. A single and familiar consideration must suffice.

Any year may be our last,—*this* year as likely as any other. And whenever death does come, the only shield against its terrors, and the only solace for mourners, is to be found in the relations the departing spirit has sustained to the Lord Jesus Christ. It is a most significant tribute which the world pays to the value of true piety, that it lays more stress upon the slight tokens a man may have furnished of even a transient interest in religion than upon all he was or all he did besides. It is not of a man's riches, or his enterprise, or his eloquence, or his wit, and of a woman's beauty, or her accomplishments, or the splendor of her entertainments, that we first think when they are dead or dying. Who can depict the remorse and dread upon a bed of sickness of those faithless disciples who, professing to be servants of the Lord Jesus Christ, have given their time, and money, and strength to the world that crucified Him! When a professing Christian of this type is struck down by a threatening illness, conscience is very apt to demand a hearing; and *now* it must and *will* be heard. "Alas, alas, I have betrayed my Master. Wearing his livery, I have consorted with his foes. Pledged to enlist other perishing sinners in his cause, I have taught them, by my example, to regard Him as a hard Master. When I first took my seat at his table I supposed I had some of the marks of true discipleship. But these have all been obliterated by my career of worldliness, and how *can* He forgive me? Mercy, mercy; God have mercy upon my soul!"

Is this overdrawn? Do you not believe it is the history of countless death-beds? And is such a death to be coveted? Even if you yourself might have the courage to dare it, what an unkindness to your friends to oblige them, after you are gone, to look with painful scrutiny through your life and character, in order to glean, if possible, some scraps of evidence upon which to found a hope that you have been saved, although 'as by fire.' You owe it to those who love you to spare them this cruel trial. And if you owe it to *them*, what do you not owe to Him who submitted to the sharpness of death, clothed with *all* its horrors, in order that you and I might die in peace?

You *may* die in peace. Take this Scripture, which is tendered you to-day, "Whose I am, and whom I serve." 'Bind it for a sign upon your hands, and let it be as frontlets between your eyes; write it upon the posts of your house, and upon your gates;' walk by the light of it, and rejoice in the liberty and strength which are bound up in it, and you *will* die in peace. Nor this alone. Should it please God to put this text into every one of our hearts, and keep alive its inspiration within us, what a year of blessing would this be to our Church! The indolent and indifferent would bring forth their buried talents and become workers; and the workers would work with lighter hearts. Those who have loved their money more than they have loved Christ would emulate the *Magi* in hastening to lay their treasures at His feet. New energy would be infused into the Sunday-schools, the missionary schemes, and all the benevolent operations with which we have to do. In place of the languor which possibly may have settled down upon us, the entire Church would soon reveal the glow of a healthful activity, and we might expect to see a blessed ingathering into the fold of those who are now far from God.

These, and such as these, are the results to be reasonably anticipated, if, with one heart and soul, and with a devout sense of our dependence upon the Divine Spirit, we accept it as our motto for the year, and faithfully live by it, "WHOSE I AM, AND WHOM I SERVE."

In the spirit of this Scripture, and with all the sympathy of which a pastor's heart is capable, alike in your joys and in your sorrows, I wish you a very happy New Year!

www.ingramcontent.com/pod-product-compliance
Lightning Source LLC
Chambersburg PA
CBHW031945230426
43672CB00010B/2051